# COOL TECH

## GADGETS, GAMES, ROBOTS, AND THE DIGITAL WORLD

London, New York,
Melbourne, Munich, and Delhi

**Senior editor** Francesca Baines
**Senior art editor** Smiljka Surla

**Editors** Clare Hibbert, James Mitchem
**Art editors** Angela Ball, Dave Ball, Daniela Boraschi

**Managing editor** Linda Esposito
**Managing art editor** Jim Green
**Category publisher** Laura Buller

**Illustrators** James Carey, I Love Dust, Infomen, Charis Tsevis
**Picture researcher** Sarah Smithies

**Senior production controller** Angela Graef
**Production editor** Andy Hilliard

**Jacket designer** Neal Cobourne
**Jacket editor** Matilda Gollen
**Development editor** Jayne Miller
**Design development manager** Sophia M. Tampakopoulos Turner

First published in the United States in 2011 by
DK Publishing
375 Hudson Street
New York, New York 10014

Copyright © 2011 Dorling Kindersley Limited

11 12 13 14 15 10 9 8 7 6 5 4 3 2 1
001 – 179073 – 05/11

A catalog record for this book is available from the Library of Congress.

ISBN: 978-0-7566-8270-5

DK books are available at special discounts when purchased in bulk for sales
promotions, premiums, fund-raising, or educational use. For details, contact:
DK Publishing Special Markets, 375 Hudson Street, New York, New York 10014
or SpecialSales@dk.com.

Hi-res workflow proofed by MDP, UK
Printed and bound by Toppan, China

Discover more at
**www.dk.com**

# COOL TECH

## GADGETS, GAMES, ROBOTS, AND THE DIGITAL WORLD

Written by **Clive Gifford**

Consultant **Dr. Mike Goldsmith**

# Contents

621.381
GIF
2011

# Calculators and
# computers

"I wish to God these calculations had been executed by steam," Charles Babbage exclaimed, poring over a mistake-filled volume of mathematical tables. The year was 1821, when such books were the only help for number-crunchers. So Babbage set out to mechanize how these tables were produced, and along the way became the first computing pioneer.

### Charles Babbage

Having taught himself algebra as a child, English inventor Charles Babbage (1791–1871) was a highly regarded mathematician by his twenties. In 1828, he was awarded the Lucasian Chair of Mathematics at Cambridge, a distinguished position held earlier by Sir Isaac Newton. Babbage would later invent lighthouse signaling devices and cowcatchers for steam trains. He also became a master code maker and breaker and an expert economist.

### The Difference Engine

In 1823, the British government gave Babbage the go-ahead to start work on a machine for calculating mathematical tables. He designed two giant calculators, called Difference Engines, the first of which (left) required 25,000 iron and brass parts! With no electricity, both machines were designed to be powered by hand.

## Birth of the computer

In the 1830s, Babbage abandoned his first Difference Engine to devote his attention to an even more ambitious plan, as shown in this complex design from 1840 (left). His steam-driven, mechanical Analytical Engine was to be a general purpose "computer," capable of all kinds of calculations, and directed by programmed instructions. Conceived decades before the invention of electronics, it was utterly revolutionary and uncannily like the design of modern computers.

## ↗ How it worked

The Analytical Engine was never actually made. If it had been, it would have been programmable using punched cards.

● The "mill" was the central processor where arithmetic was performed. It retrieved and executed instructions and data from the "store" just like a modern computer.

● The "store" was the engine's expandable memory, capable of holding results and data during calculations.

● Results could be sent to the engine's own printer and graph plotter or onto punched cards.

> "Babbage's reputation has been vindicated, both as a visionary of the computer age and, more specifically, as an engineer of the most extraordinary caliber."
>
> Doron Swade, curator of the Science Museum, London

## Failure

Babbage's engines were not completed in his lifetime. The sheer ambition of his designs, his perfectionism, disputes over costs, a struggle for funds, and problems engineering the highly accurate parts required (above) were the main reasons for this failure. "Another age must be the judge," Babbage admitted.

## Did you know?

Almost 200 years after Babbage was born, the Science Museum in London built his second Difference Engine using the original blueprints. It has more than 4,000 parts, and what's more, it works!

## The countess

Daughter of the poet Lord Byron, English mathematician Augusta Ada King, Countess of Lovelace, first met Babbage in 1833. Translating an article about his work in 1842–3, her notes included algorithms (instructions for solving mathematical problems) that effectively make her one of the first programmers. A 1979 computer language was named Ada in her honor.

# The great brain

It is 1947, and the world's first general-purpose electronic computer is at work, churning through top secret calculations for the American hydrogen bomb program. Dubbed the "great brain" by the press, the Electronic Numerical Integrator and Computer (ENIAC) weighed in at 60,000 lb (27,000 kg) and consumed as much power as 15,000 iPads. At the machine's heart lay vacuum tubes—electrical components able to act as switches (that break or make electrical circuits) or amplify switches. A radio of the time might contain 10 vacuum tubes, but this beast boasted 17,468 of them.

## Building ENIAC

J. Presper Eckert (right) was just out of his teens when he and Dr. John Mauchly began work on ENIAC. Completed in 1945, ENIAC ran for a decade. Eckert and Mauchly also formed their own company to produce UNIVAC I, the first computer to go on sale to the public in the United States.

## Did you know?

To figure out which type of wire to use to build ENIAC, J. Presper Eckert starved lab rats for a few days. Then he gave them samples of different types of cable to determine which they gnawed through the least.

## Massive machine

No wonder ENIAC took three years to build. It was 98 ft (30 m) long, more than 10 ft (3 m) high, and 3 ft (1 m) deep. Its 40 front panels, which were arranged in a U shape, required hundreds of thousands of hand-soldered joints.

## Women's work

Six female mathematicians programmed ENIAC. Their job title was "Computer." Although ENIAC worked quickly, changing its program could be tedious because its panels had to be rewired, a process that could take up to two days.

## Shrunk on silicon

From ENIAC onward, computers advanced rapidly and their speed accelerated as their components shrank in size. In 1997, students at the University of Pennsylvania re-created ENIAC on just one silicon chip (left). While ENIAC could perform 5,000 operations per second, an Intel Core Duo chip today can manage 21.6 billion.

"We're flooding people with information. We need to feed it through a processor. A human must turn information into intelligence or knowledge. We've tended to forget that no computer will ever ask a new question."

*Grace Hopper*

A gifted mathematician, Grace Hopper (1906–92) joined the navy during World War II. There, she became the first woman to program the Harvard Mark I, a pioneering computer based at Harvard University. Then, in 1949, Hopper joined the Eckert-Mauchly Corporation and worked on the first commercial computer, UNIVAC I. Her greatest contributions, however, came in the 1950s. She developed the first compilers, progams that made programming far easier, and also worked on the first high-level computer language for business, the Common Business-Oriented Language (COBOL), still in use today.

**Did you know?**
Hopper popularized the terms "bug" and "debugging" (to remove errors in computer code) after an incident when a moth was trapped inside part of a computer at Harvard.

# Evolution of the computer

Computers took a long time coming. They developed out of centuries of attempts at getting machines to help perform complex calculations. A burst of innovation before, during, and after World War II led to the arrivals of the jet engine, the atomic bomb, and the first practical computers. In the decades since then, computers have advanced at a spectacular rate.

**↑ 1642**
Blaise Pascal creates the Pascaline, one of the first mechanical adding machines.

**1936**
Alan Turing develops the concept of a theoretical computing machine.

**↓ 1952**
Tom Cranston and Fred Longstaff invent the trackball input device, using a bowling ball at the center of their apparatus.

**1946**
J. Presper Eckert and John Mauchly complete the Electronic Numerical Integrator and Computer (ENIAC). It is one of the first digital computers.

**↓ 1822**
Charles Babbage begins work on his Difference Engine.

**↑ 1939–45**
In the United States, Britain, and Germany, mechanical and electric calculators and computer-style machines, such as the Harvard Mark I (above), are developed. They crack codes, calculate firing tables for artillery, and help in other ways with the war effort.

**↑ 3000 BCE**
The abacus is invented in Babylonia.

**1938**
In Berlin, Germany, Konrad Zuse completes the first binary programmable mechanical computer, the Z1. His Z3, the first true electronic computer, follows in 1941.

**1946**
John von Neumann proposes that a program can be stored in a computer the same way data is. His proposal of "von Neumann architecture" for computers becomes the basis for modern machines.

**1952**
Grace Hopper and her team complete the first compiler, a program that allows a computer operator to use words instead of numbers.

**1623**
Wilhelm Schickard invents the mechanical calculator.

**1854**
The English philosopher George Boole develops Boolean logic and algebra, using binary numbers (ones and zeroes)—the basis of modern computer logic.

**↓ 1890**
This year's U.S. Census is completed in record time thanks to Herman Hollerith's invention of an automated tabulating machine, using punched cards as storage. Hollerith's company merges with others in 1911 to form IBM.

**↓ 1956**
The first hard disk drive, the IBM Model 350 Disk File, goes on sale with the IBM 305 RAMAC computer. It weighs around a ton and holds up to 5 MB of data. Users can rent 1 MB of storage on the device for $130 a month.

**↓ 1666**
Samuel Morland produces a pocket-sized mechanical calculator capable of addition and subtraction.

**↑ 1939**
Hewlett-Packard is founded in a garage in Palo Alto, California. Eight models of its first product, a sound generator, are bought by Walt Disney for its 1940 movie *Fantasia*.

**1948**
The first computer to store its programs and data in electronic memory, the Manchester Baby, begins operation. The following year, it is upgraded with magnetic-drum storage to become the Manchester Mark I.

## Rich Skrenta

As a 15-year-old in 1982, Rich Skrenta created Elk Cloner, one of the first computer viruses. It was transmitted on floppy disks between early Apple computers. Skrenta went on to work for Commodore, Sun Microsystems, and AOL. He helped form the Open Directory Project (a collection of World Wide Web links) and, in 2010, launched a major new search engine, Blekko.

"This is only a foretaste of what is to come, and only the shadow of what is going to be... I do not see why [computers] should not enter any of the fields normally covered by the human intellect."

**Alan Turing,** *1949. Turing (1912–1954) was an English mathematician and cryptanalyst (code breaker), and one of the founders of modern computer science.*

---

**↓ 1964**
John Kemeny and Thomas Kurtz develop the BASIC (Beginner's All-purpose Symbolic Instruction Code) programming language, which will drive the first boom of home computers in the 1970s and '80s.

**← 1971**
The Intel 4004 microprocessor chip, designed by Ted Hoff, is the first complete central processing unit (CPU).

**↑ 1982**
The Commodore C64 home computer is released. It goes on to sell 22 million units, far more than any other single model of personal computer.

**↓ 1968**
Douglas Engelbart demonstrates the mouse (first built in 1963), hypertext, and on-screen video conferencing in a multimedia demonstration.

**↑ 1993**
Intel releases the first Pentium microprocessor chip.

**1961**
Jack Kilby and Robert Noyce develop the silicon chip, laying many integrated circuits on a single wafer of silicon.

**↑ 1977**
Radio Shack unveils its fully assembled microcomputer, the TRS-80 Model I, with keyboard, monitor, and cassette unit.

**1978**
VisiCalc, the first automatic recalculating spreadsheet software for personal computers, is released.

**↑ 1984**
Apple advertise their Macintosh computer, the first big-selling computer with a graphic user interface and a mouse.

**↓ 1996**
The Universal Serial Bus (USB) 1.0 standard is established, allowing different makes of peripherals to communicate with computers. The faster USB 2.0 is introduced four years later.

---

**1963**
ASCII, the American Standard Code for Information Interchange, is announced. It allows computers from different manufacturers to exchange data.

**1969**
Gary Starkweather, a researcher at Xerox, invents the laser printer. IBM will sell the first laser printer, the 3800, from 1975 onward.

**↓ 1981**
IBM launches its Personal Computer (PC). It sells more than three million units and its operating system, MS-DOS, becomes the standard for business programs.

**1985**
Aldus announces its PageMaker program for use on Macintosh computers, launching an interest in desktop publishing.

**2001**
Microsoft releases its Windows XP operating system. As of 2010, it powers more PCs than any other operating system.

**↓ 1965**
Digital Equipment Corp (DEC) puts on sale the first commercially successful minicomputer, the PDP-8.

**1975**
Bill Gates and Paul Allen found Microsoft.

**↓ 2007**
The first netbook, the Asus Eee PC 701, goes on sale in October. More than 300,000 are sold before the end of the year.

**1976**
Steve Jobs, Steve Wozniak, and Ronald Wayne found Apple Computer, a company to sell their Apple I computer.

**1991**
A Finnish college student, Linus Torvalds, begins building Linux, a free operating system for PCs. It goes on to become the third most popular operating system family, after Windows and Mac OS. Versions of Linux are found everywhere, from smartphones and netbooks to supercomputers.

# A vision of
# the future

Every time you use a mouse to click on a link to a new web page, you have American electrical engineer Douglas Engelbart to thank. Engelbart was an early computer pioneer. As far back as 1951, he imagined screens with information flowing between them, and people navigating the screens to learn, form, and organize their ideas. Sounds familiar? He could be describing the Internet and hypertext—text with active links to other pages.

## Douglas Engelbart

Born in 1925, Engelbart studied electrical engineering. In 1957 he joined the Stanford Research Institute (SRI) in California, where he was later given his own research lab. There, his team developed the revolutionary oNLine System (NLS). This allowed up to 16 workstations to operate together, running programs with multiple windows between which text and objects could move.

## New controls

In the early 1950s, very few computers existed, and they were controlled by experts and engineers using punched cards or rewiring circuits. Engelbart's vision demanded faster, simpler, more natural ways of working. His team developed cursors that could be dragged around the screen. They also experimented with chorded keysets (keyboards), where pressing down different combinations of five pianolike keys created commands.

## First mouse

In 1963, Engelbart and a colleague, Bill English, invented the first computer mouse. The name came from the tail-like cable that ran from the back of the wooden box. Known more formally as an "X-Y position indicator for a display system," the device had a single click switch and two metal wheels positioned at 90-degree angles to each other that kept track of up-and-down and side-to-side movement. Computer mice only became popular 20 years later.

San Francisco, 1968

At a conference in 1968, Engelbart gave a demonstration to 1,000 computer experts that would make them think about computers in a totally new way. In what became known as the "mother of all demos," his presentation included:

● Documents being edited in multiple windows by different people on different computers.

● The computer mouse, word processing, instant messaging, and hypertext between documents, files, and programs.

● Real-time video conferencing between Engelbart and employees at his laboratory approximately 37 miles (60 km) away (above).

> "Computer technology is going to blossom so spectacularly, and hit our society so hard, that I am both thrilled and frightened... Imagine what it might be like to have information-handling 'horsepower' available for your personal use."
>
> *Douglas Engelbart, 1961*

### Inspirational teacher

Engelbart's work has won more than 30 awards, including the $500,000 Lemelson–MIT Prize (1997) and the National Medal of Technology (2000), which was presented by President Bill Clinton. Over his career, Engelbart influenced many other computing pioneers, including those he collaborated with on early Internet projects. Some of Engelbart's employees went on to the Xerox PARC research facility, where they developed the first graphical user interfaces, allowing users to interact with systems by clicking on icons instead of typing in commands.

## ZX81 →

In 1981, British inventor Clive Sinclair released the ZX81. It had a mere 1 KB of memory, featured a barely usable keyboard, and had to be hooked up to a television to display its black-and-white text and rudimentary graphics, but it was a revelation. The ZX81's launch price was just £69.99 in the UK and $99.99 in the United States. Computers had never been so affordable before.

## Commodore 64 →

By 1982, the home-computer market was starting to mature. One of the most popular computers of the time was the Commodore 64. The C64 had a full keyboard, a then-enormous 64 KB of internal memory, a built-in sound synthesizer, and more advanced graphics than any of its rivals.

## ← Spectrum

Sinclair's successor to the ZX81, the Spectrum, released in 1982, had a rubber-key keyboard, 16 or 48 KB of memory, and color graphics. It was still primitive, but a growing band of computer enthusiasts wrote all kinds of software for it, including games such as *Horace Goes Skiing* and *Chuckie Egg*, and astronomy and accounting packages.

# Early home computing

In the mid-1970s, only a handful of electronics enthusiasts owned computers, which they had built from kits. Then, starting in the late 1970s, affordable microcomputers gave millions of people their first direct taste of computing. The boom spawned numerous cottage industries in computer books, magazines, software, and games.

## TRS-80 →

Priced at $600 and including a black-and-white monitor, the TRS-80 went on sale in 3,000 Radio Shack and Tandy stores in December 1977. More than 400,000 machines were sold, along with business software such as *Payroll* and *Statistical Analysis*, and, of course, games. A color version of the computer, the TRS-80 CoCo, followed three years later.

## ← BASIC

Computer owners of the 1970s and early '80s often wrote their own programs using an instruction language known as BASIC. It had easy-to-learn commands, such as IF-THEN decision statements and GOTO to navigate to a numbered line of program code. Many of today's tech experts learned their trade on this surprisingly flexible computer language.

## Dot-matrix printer →

Despite the noisy clatter it made during operation, the dot-matrix printer was the must-have computing accessory of the early 1980s. Characters were formed from a series of tightly packed dots printed by pins striking an ink ribbon. Compared to today's printers, however, output was slow (50 to 300 characters per second).

## ↓ IBM PC

The first IBM (International Business Machines) personal computer, the model 5150, arrived in 1981. Launch prices in the United States ranged from $1,565 to $3,000. The 5150 stored data on cassettes or floppy disks, boasting an Intel processor and the Microsoft Disk Operating System (MS-DOS), designed by Bill Gates. The computer was powerful enough for small businesses as well as personal use.

## ← Acoustic coupler

Few home computers went online in the early 1980s. The acoustic coupler was one of the first devices that made it possible. It converted computer data into audio signals that could be sent and received on a phone line. Most couplers ran at a speed of about 300 bits per second—at that rate, downloading a 9 MB music file would have taken almost 3 days!

## ← Floppy drives

Many early home computers relied on audio cassette tapes to store and load programs. However, a cassette recorder could take 5 to 10 minutes to load a single program into memory. Floppy disks, developed by IBM in 1971, offered far more convenient storage. They were flat magnetic disks, protected by a flexible plastic cover.

**Acer Aspire One 751**

# Connectivity

The laptop can be connected to external devices such as speakers, printers, and cameras via a range of ports (sockets). A built-in card reader allows users to transfer data and images using memory cards.

### 1 Shell
The outer casing of this computer is molded from plastic, though others are formed from light metals such as aluminum. Reducing weight and bulk are priorities in the design of laptops, so many, like this one, come without a built-in DVD drive.

### 2 LCD Screen
Computer screens are measured diagonally and in inches. This laptop has an 11.6 in (29.4 cm) screen and is a liquid crystal display (LCD), backlit by a lamp shining through the liquid cells out towards the user.

### 3 Keyboard
All computers need input devices for users to enter data or commands. Keys on a keyboard are switches, completing an electrical circuit when they are pressed, sending that key's signal to the processor.

### 4 Motherboard
The main circuit board houses the body of the computer—its central processor, internal system memory, system clock, and, if the machine has integrated graphics, the graphics processors that handle the display.

### 5 Hard Drive
These magnetic storage devices are made up of a series of thin metal plates attached to a spindle and electric motor that spins them around at high speed, ranging from 5,400 to 10,000 revolutions per minute.

### 6 Heat Sink
The processor in a computer generates a lot of heat, that can threaten performance and reliability. A heat sink transfers much of the heat away from the processor into the surrounding air, sometimes assisted by a cooling fan.

### 7 Battery
The single heaviest part of most portable computers, a notebook's battery is rechargeable. This six-cell lithium-ion battery powers the machine for up to seven hours.

Touch pad supports page flick gesture

3

USB port to connect a range of devices

LED power board with 5-in-1 card reader

4

5

6

7

Frame to keep the LCD screen in place

2 ↓

0.3 megapixel webcam for video chat

*"We now have mobile computers that you can use to edit video, play DVDs, rip CDs, and develop software on— something that would have been a fantasy only a decade ago."*
Jonathan Bray, 2007

Jonathan Bray is a British technology writer and former deputy editor of *PC Pro* magazine.

## Components

**Processor**
A CPU (central processing unit) is the computer's brain. It is capable of performing the machine's calculations at rates measured in millions per second. The Atom Z520 processor used in the Aspire One is common in many small, lightweight netbooks.

**RAM**
Random access memory (RAM) is a circuit that holds data and gives the computer's processor, and any running programs, their own area in which to perform and store processes and data.

# Laptop

Laptops and their smaller, lighter, and usually less powerful cousins, netbooks, allow people to keep in touch, work, learn, or play when on the move. They take up little space, yet the most powerful can compete in performance with many far-bulkier desktop machines. Early portable computers with only a fraction of the capability of a modern machine often weighed more than 22 lb (10 kg). The Acer Aspire One 751 featured here weighs a mere 2.7 lb (1.25 kg).

# Networks

A computer network involves two or more computers, known as nodes, linked so that they can communicate electronically with each other. Networks can be wired, with cables physically connecting the computers, or wireless, with radio waves or satellite signals linking them. Once connected, computers can exchange data, including sound and image files.

## ISPs

In return for a monthly or annual fee, an Internet Service Provider (ISP) provides millions of businesses and homes with Internet access via telephone, cable, or satellite links. The first public ISP was TheWorld, which was started in 1989 in Brookline, Massachusetts.

## Home networks

A typical home computer network might consist of two or three PCs that share a printer, scanner, or a large hard drive for backup storage. Each device has its own network address so that other devices can identify and communicate with it using rules called protocols.

## LANs and WANs

A typical office has a number of machines networked over a small area. The above office LAN (Local Area Network) may use a router to connect to other nearby LANs. A number of LANs may connect to form a WAN (Wide Area Network), which operates over great distances.

## Satellites

Satellites orbiting the Earth can relay data to and from computers to enable access to the Internet. This is particularly valuable in rural communities with no access to cable networks. All users need is a dish placed in unobstructed view of the skyline in order to access the Internet directly.

### Did you know?

The Virtual Internet Cafe opened in 2008. Based online, it allows users to control its computers remotely so that they can surf the Internet without exposing their own PCs to malware.

## Around the world

The Internet is the biggest WAN of all. It consists of vast numbers of networks— from small LANs to huge academic or governmental networks—all linked together using common protocols. Many ISPs' networks interconnect at locations called access points or Internet exchanges.

### Did you know?

The first "Internet café in a box" was installed in Zambia by the Computer Aid charity in 2010. A shipping container was fitted with 11 computers powered by solar panels on the container's roof.

## Cybercafes

The first Internet café opened in San Francisco in 1991. For a purchase of food or drink or a small fee, cybercafes offer use of a computer connected to the Internet, or a Wi-Fi hotspot for your own PC. In countries with low computer ownership, most people access the Net in cafés.

**High School**

## Server network

The computers in this school network are linked to a central computer, called a server, which controls some tasks, such as printing, on behalf of the other computers, called clients. This is a client-server network. An alternative is a peer-to-peer network where all the computers perform the same range of tasks.

**Café**

# Inventing the
# World Wide Web

On December 25, 1990, Tim Berners-Lee set a new task for a computer at the European Organization for Nuclear Research (CERN) laboratory in Switzerland. The computer was a prototype web server. It hosted the world's first web page, which described the World Wide Web and showed others how to start their own websites. Before this event, the Internet was the mostly text-based domain of scientists and other academics.

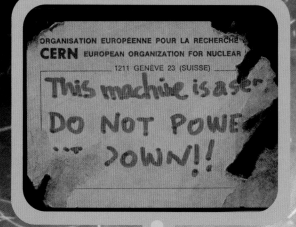

## ENQUIRE

In 1980, Berners-Lee wrote a program called ENQUIRE for use inside CERN to track the connections between different people and projects using hyperlinks (see pages 16–17). Ten years later, he would use similar principles to create a web of hyperlinked documents on the Internet—the World Wide Web. This was first hosted on a single computer on which Berners-Lee scrawled on the back: "This machine is a server. Do not power it down."

### Did you know?

In a 2009 interview in the London *Times*, Berners-Lee admitted that the "//" (two forward slashes) in web addresses had not really been necessary. "There you go—it seemed like a good idea at the time," he joked.

### Early education

Tim Berners-Lee was born in England in 1955. His parents, Conway and Mary Berners-Lee, had met three years earlier at Ferranti, where they both worked as mathematicians on the Mark 1 computer. Tim studied physics at Oxford, where he built his own first computer from some logic gates, an M6800 processor, and old television parts. Berners-Lee followed his parents' footsteps and began working as a software consultant at CERN in 1980.

Document Title: NCSA Mosaic Home Page
Document URL: http://www.ncsa.uiuc.edu/SDG/Software/Mosaic/NCSAMosaicHome.html

# N C S A
# MOSAIC
X Window System • Microsoft Windows • Macintosh

Welcome to NCSA Mosaic, an Internet information browser and World Wide Web client. NCSA Mosaic was developed at the National Center for Supercomputing Applications at the University of Illinois in --> Urbana-Champaign. NCSA Mosaic software is copyrighted by The Board of Trustees of the University of Illinois (UI), and ownership remains with the UI.

Jan '97
The Software Development Group at NCSA has worked on NCSA Mosaic for nearly four years and we've learned a lot in the process. We are honored that we were able to help bring this technology to the masses and appreciated all the support and feedback we have received in return. However, the time has come for us to concentrate our limited resources in other areas of interest and development on Mosaic is complete.

All information about the Mosaic project is available from the homepages.

NCSA Mosaic Platforms:
● NCSA Mosaic for the X Window System
● NCSA Mosaic for the Apple Macintosh
NCSA Mosaic for Microsoft Windows

## W3C

In 1994, Berners-Lee moved to head the World Wide Web Consortium (W3C), a group devoted to improving the Web. He campaigned hard to keep the Web open and free. Nearly 20 years later, he is still a director of the W3C, as well as a respected advisor and researcher for governments and academic bodies.

## Browsers

One boost to the early World Wide Web was the development of new, more user- and graphics-friendly browser programs (see panel, right). Marc Andreessen and colleagues at the University of Illinois developed the Mosaic browser, which became available in 1993. Mosaic helped popularize browsing, and the number of websites started to mushroom.

"The Web as I envisaged it, we have not seen it yet. The future is still so much bigger than the past."
*Tim Berners-Lee, 2009*

## ↗ The invention of the Web

In the late 1980s, Berners-Lee proposed building a hyperlink-based information system for use over the Internet. Working with a Belgian computer engineer, Robert Cailliau (above left, displaying the first server computer in the museum at CERN) and others, Berners-Lee had to assemble a number of different elements to get the World Wide Web up and running:

● **HTML** Berners-Lee needed a standard language to create hypertext documents that could be retrieved and viewed on different computers all over the world. The answer was hypertext markup language (HTML), which uses tags as instructions, allowing pages to display different text sizes and colors, along with pictures and other files.

● **HTTP** The team developed the hypertext transfer protocol (HTTP), a system that allowed computers to send hypertext documents over the Internet.

● **Browser** Berners-Lee and his colleagues created the first web browser—a program that could find, retrieve, and view hypertext documents. Initially called "WorldWideWeb," it was renamed "Nexus" to avoid confusion with the Web itself.

● **Web server** The software that stores web pages on a computer and makes them available to others—a server—had to be created. In 1990, Berners-Lee set up the first web server at CERN with the address "http://info.cern.ch."

## Web explosion

The World Wide Web became available over the Internet in August 1991, with just one server hosting a single website. Ten years later, there were 36 million websites and, by 2011, more than 250 million. This boom was helped early on by CERN's decision to make the World Wide Web free for use by everyone.

# Undersea cables

In a secret location, buried 6 ft (2 m) beneath the sands of a beach—possibly this beach—in Cornwall, on the western tip of England, lies a $400 million cable not much thicker than a garden hose. This high-capacity Internet cable links New York and London, the busiest hubs in the world. In fact, around 90 percent of global Internet traffic is carried by a vast cable network that snakes over land and sea, with more than 500,000 miles (800,000 km) of cable found underwater.

**Top secret**
The location of the British beach the cable passes under is a secret. The cabling station, just set back from the beach, does not appear on any map.

**High speed**
It takes a fraction of a second for data to travel the 7,600-mile (12,200 km) round trip from England to the United States. About every 30 miles (49 km) or so, the signals get a boost from amplifier devices called repeaters. Each repeater costs around $1.5 million.

**Did you know?**
When the first transatlantic fiber-optic cables were laid in the 1980s, they attracted sharks, resulting in severed cables and electrocuted sharks. The cables were quickly enclosed in a protective casing.

## Making repairs

The robot below is being
lowered into the sea where it
will crawl the seabed repairing
damaged cables. In 2009,
millions of Internet users in
India saw their connections
wiped out after a ship's anchor
cut a cable. If a cable breaks,
data is usually rerouted until
repairs are completed.

## Fiber optics

Bundled inside the main transatlantic
cable, the OALC-4 SPDA, are eight
fiber-optic cables, each the width of
a single human hair and with enough
bandwidth for 20 million people. In the
United States, the cables emerge from
beneath the Atlantic Ocean at a vast
server center that channels the data
to around 150 countries.

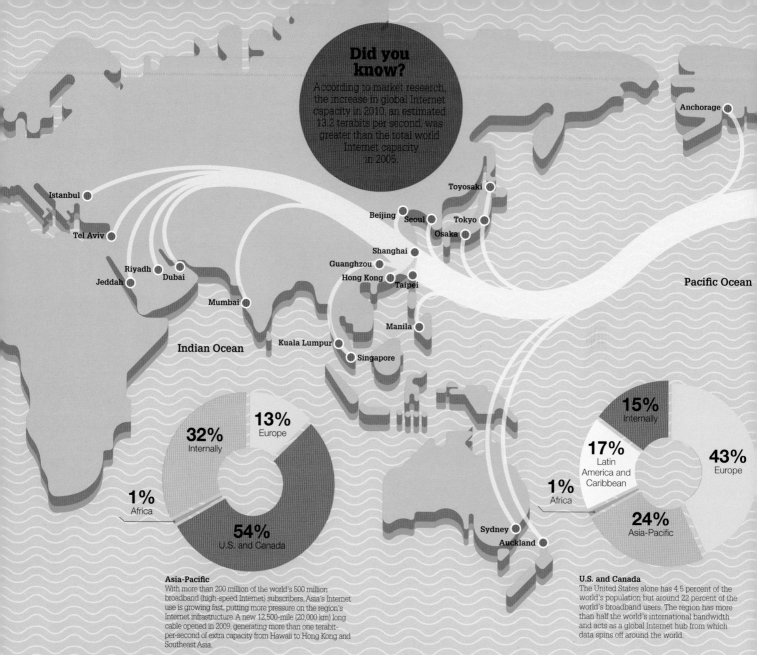

Anchorage

Istanbul

Tel Aviv

Riyadh

Jeddah    Dubai

Mumbai

Toyosaki

Beijing    Seoul    Tokyo

Osaka

Shanghai

Guanghzou

Hong Kong    Taipei

Manila

Kuala Lumpur

Singapore

**Indian Ocean**

**Pacific Ocean**

Sydney

Auckland

### Asia-Pacific pie chart
- **13%** Europe
- **32%** Internally
- **1%** Africa
- **54%** U.S. and Canada

**Asia-Pacific**
With more than 200 million of the world's 500 million broadband (high-speed Internet) subscribers, Asia's Internet use is growing fast, putting more pressure on the region's Internet infrastructure. A new 12,500-mile (20,000 km) long cable opened in 2009, generating more than one terabit-per-second of extra capacity from Hawaii to Hong Kong and Southeast Asia.

### U.S. and Canada pie chart
- **15%** Internally
- **17%** Latin America and Caribbean
- **1%** Africa
- **24%** Asia-Pacific
- **43%** Europe

**U.S. and Canada**
The United States alone has 4.5 percent of the world's population but around 22 percent of the world's broadband users. The region has more than half the world's international bandwidth and acts as a global Internet hub from which data spins off around the world.

## Global data capacity

This map shows the approximate data capacity or bandwidth between many of the world's busiest cities, major Internet hubs such as London, New York, and Shanghai. The circular charts detail what percentage of a region's bandwidth is connected to other regions.

# Internet traffic

When you click on a link to visit a website, your request and the web page you eventually see have traveled as data, a tiny part of the vast flow of data over worldwide Internet networks. The measure of how much data can be sent over a network at once is called the bandwidth of the connection. As more and more people get connected, Internet traffic continues to rise. In 2009 alone, it increased by 74 percent, and then by an additional 62 percent in 2010. The Internet's infrastructure must continue to grow to cope with this ever-increasing demand.

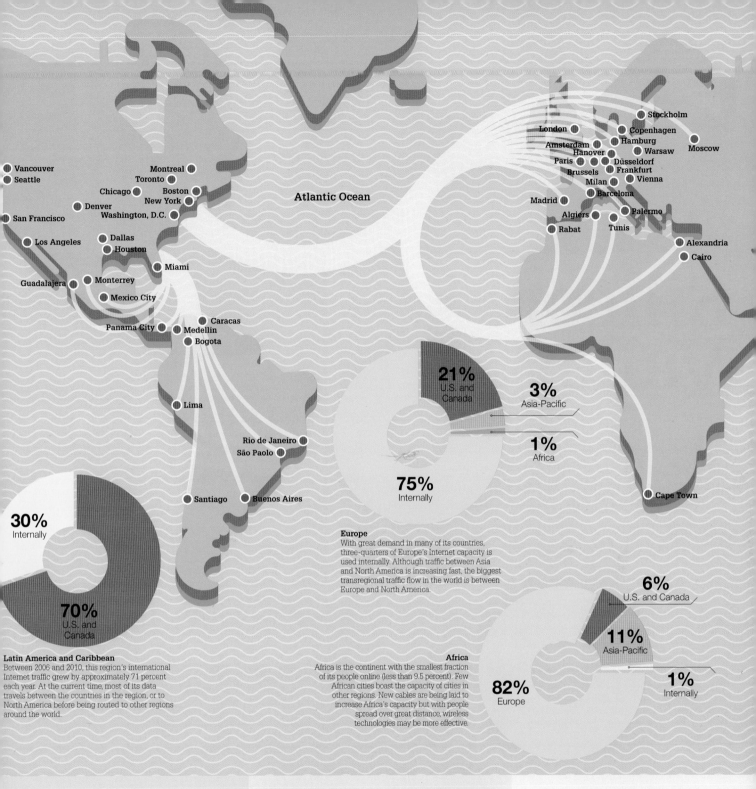

**Atlantic Ocean**

Vancouver
Seattle
Montreal
Toronto
Chicago    Boston
Denver    New York
San Francisco    Washington, D.C.
Los Angeles    Dallas
Houston
Miami
Guadalajera    Monterrey
Mexico City
Panama City    Caracas
Medellin
Bogota
Lima
Rio de Janeiro
São Paolo
Santiago    Buenos Aires

Stockholm
London    Copenhagen
Amsterdam    Hamburg
Hanover    Warsaw    Moscow
Paris    Düsseldorf
Brussels    Frankfurt
Milan    Vienna
Barcelona
Madrid
Algiers    Palermo
Rabat    Tunis
Alexandria
Cairo
Cape Town

**21%**
U.S. and Canada

**3%**
Asia-Pacific

**1%**
Africa

**75%**
Internally

**Europe**
With great demand in many of its countries, three-quarters of Europe's Internet capacity is used internally. Although traffic between Asia and North America is increasing fast, the biggest transregional traffic flow in the world is between Europe and North America.

**30%**
Internally

**70%**
U.S. and Canada

**Latin America and Caribbean**
Between 2006 and 2010, this region's international Internet traffic grew by approximately 71 percent each year. At the current time, most of its data travels between the countries in the region, or to North America before being routed to other regions around the world.

**Africa**
Africa is the continent with the smallest fraction of its people online (less than 9.5 percent). Few African cities boast the capacity of cities in other regions. New cables are being laid to increase Africa's capacity but with people spread over great distance, wireless technologies may be more effective.

**6%**
U.S. and Canada

**11%**
Asia-Pacific

**1%**
Internally

**82%**
Europe

## Miami gateway

Around 90 percent of all Internet traffic between North America and Latin America goes through one building in downtown Miami. The Terremark data center is an Internet exchange filled with thousands of server computers. They are protected by round-the-clock security and 7 in (18 cm) thick walls capable of withstanding a hurricane.

**Did you know?**
More than 160 different cable networks meet and run through the Terremark building in Miami. On its roof are mounted two 52 ft (16 m) satellite dishes and and one 45 ft (14m) dish.

**← Hewlett Packard (H**
In 1938, two Stanford engineering graduates, B Hewlett and Dave Packar began work in this garag in Palo Alto. HP is now or of the largest information technology companies.

# Silicon Valley

It all started here. A stretch of land south of San Francisco, California, became home to the greatest concentration of computing and high-tech pioneers ever known. Named Silicon Valley, after the material that is used in computer electronics, the headquarters of many huge Internet and computing companies are found in the area.

**← Intel**
Intel was founded by three former Fairchild engineers in 1968 to build memory chips. By 1992, Intel was the world's largest semiconductor company, famous for supplying the processor chips inside IBM PCs.

## Apples to Apple

Once full of apple orchards and known as "The Valley of Heart's Delight," the Silicon Valley region includes the Santa Clara Valley and the city of San Jose. In the 1950s, several high-tech companies moved their research bases to the area, and a group of engineers formed Fairchild Semiconductor, which pioneered computer-circuit technology. By 1972, more than 60 electronics companies were based in the valley, most formed by ex-Fairchild employees. Four years later, Apple made its home here, too.

# SanDisk

## Headquarters

**← Facebook**
Facebook began as a social networking site used by students of Harvard University. In 2004, it moved west and made its headquarters in Palo Alto.

**facebook**
**1601 California Ave.**

**PARC →**
In 1970, Xerox opened the Palo Alto Research Center (PARC), a high-tech research and development base. Optical discs, laser printing, and user interfaces such as Windows all first came from this Silicon Valley–based think tank.

**parc**
Palo Alto Research Center
3333 COYOTE HILL ROAD

**Symantec →**
Gary Hendrix worked at SRI before founding a company that became Symantec, the makers of Norton AntiVirus as well as other popular computer software. They are based in Mountain View, a stone's throw away from Google's headquarters.

**Symantec**
World Headquarters

**Adobe →**
Adobe was formed in 1982 by two PARC researchers who developed the key language for printers. Seven years later, Adobe released the image-editing software Photoshop. In 1993, Adobe introduced the famous PDF file format.

**Adobe**

# Heavy hitters

Dozens of high-tech companies have bases in Silicon Valley, from Adobe to Yahoo! This is partly due to ex-employees of one company forming their own nearby, such as former Apple employee Trip Hawkins, who went on to found Electronic Arts, one of the first home-computer-game companies, in 1982.

**YAHOO!**

**← Yahoo!**
In 1994, two Stanford University students created a website called "David and Jerry's Guide to the World Wide Web." This became Yahoo!, which made a profit of $598 million in 2009.

**SUN Microsystems →**
In 1982, SUN (named after the Stanford University Network) began by making computers. In 1995, SUN produced the Java computer language, now one of the most widely used computer programming languages.

**Sun**
microsystems

**Buildings**
**15, 16**
Sun Learning Services

**4150, 4160**
Network Circle

**eBay →**
Pierre Omidyar was working as a software engineer in Silicon Valley when he began this Internet-auction website at his home in San Jose. eBay's headquarters remain in the city.

**ebay**

"I think it's fair to say that personal computers have become the most empowering tool we've ever created. They're tools of communication, they're tools of creativity, and they can be shaped by their user."

## *Bill Gates*

*Bill Gates (born 1955) is the cofounder and chairman of Microsoft, the world's largest software company. He began programming as a teenager and dropped out of college to form Microsoft in 1975. Ten years later the company launched the first version of Windows, the operating system now installed on more than 85 percent of all desktop and notebook computers. Gates is one of the world's wealthiest people and in 1994 set up a charitable organization to which he has donated more than $28 billion. The Bill and Melinda Gates Foundation is dedicated to bringing innovation in health, development, and learning in the global community.*

### Did you know?

Bill Gates has a fly named after him, in recognition of his contribution to dipterology, the science of flies. *Eristalis gatesi* is a species of flower fly that lives in the forests of Costa Rica.

# How Apple grew

Founded by Steve Jobs, Steve Wozniak, and Ronald Wayne on April 1 1976, Apple has grown from a tiny start-up in a California bedroom to a global brand that employs more than 46,000 people. In 2010, the company boasted profits of $14 billion. Famous for their design and innovation, Apple products have helped revolutionize the computing, music, and phone industries.

## Did you know?

The Apple Lisa, regarded as Apple's largest commercial failure, was named after Steve Jobs's daughter. It went on sale for a whopping $10,000.

**← 1984, Macintosh 128K**
A 9 in (23 cm) black-and-white screen was built into the first Apple Macintosh, which went on sale for $2,495.

**→ 1997, Power Mac G3**
Found in tests to be faster than rival PCs, the Power Mac was advertised on TV using snails and rabbits.

**↓ 1999, iBook**
A range of colorful laptops launched with organic, clamshell-shaped cases and built-in handles.

**↓ 1976, First Apple computer**
Only 200 Apple Is were ever built, and now they're collector's items. They cost $666.66 new, but in 2010 one sold at auction for $178,000.

**↓ 1991, PowerBook 100**
Weighing just over 4 lb (2 kg), the slimmed-down PowerBook 100 was Apple's first successful portable computer.

**↓ 1997, 20th Anniversary Mac**
This unusual machine included a Bose sound system and built-in TV and radio. Its price tag was $10,000.

**↑ 1987, Macintosh 2**
With its separate hard drive, screen, and keyboard, this was the first modular Mac.

**↓ 1999, AirPort**
A Wi-Fi base station that created a wireless local area network that allowed Apple computers to connect to the Internet.

**↘ 1998, iMac**
The Apple iMac G3 was released in 13 different colors, including Bondi Blue, Sage, Ruby, Grape, and Blue Dalmatian.

**↘ 1989, Mac Portable**
Apple's first portable computer weighed almost 15 lb (7 kg) and was a commercial flop.

**↑ 1977, Apple II**
The first successful home computer with color graphics. Versions of the Apple II would be sold new until 1993.

**↑ 1999, Power Mac G4**
Codenamed "Yikes!" during development, this machine was one of the first PCs with a recordable DVD drive.

**← 1982, Apple Lisa**
The first Apple with a mouse and graphical user interface (GUI), the Lisa had a 5 MB external hard disk.

**↑ 1994, Power Macintosh 8100**
This range of fast Power Macintoshes was produced up until 2006.

## Steve Jobs and Steve Wozniak

Twelve days after cofounding Apple, Ronald Wayne sold his 10-percent share for just $800 (it would now be worth billions). The two Steves led Apple through its early years. Wozniak (right) stopped working full-time for Apple in 1987, but is still on the payroll. Jobs (left) departed in 1984 to buy and run Pixar, but returned to head Apple in the late 1990s.

# "Do you want to spend the rest of your life selling sugared water or do you want a chance to change the world?"

**Steve Jobs** to John Sculley (at center of picture, left), then CEO of Pepsi, trying to convince him to join Apple

**↑ 2001, PowerBook G4**
The first in a series of slimline laptops with a front-loading DVD slot and a 15 in (38 cm) screen.

**↑ 2006, Wireless Mighty Mouse**
Apple's first multibutton mouse came complete with a small internal speaker in its shell.

**2009, iPhone 3GS**
Two years after the first iPhone, the third generation arrived with more speed, 32 GB of memory, and a video camera.

**↑ 2010, iPad**
A tablet computer particularly suited to viewing multimedia apps on its multi-touch 9.8 in (25 cm) screen is launched.

**↑ 2002, The New iMac**
The successor to the original iMac had a 15 in (38 cm) color screen and an unusual domed body.

**↓ 2006, MacBook**
The first in a line of MacBook laptops that would become Apple's biggest selling family of computers.

**↑ 2008, MacBook**
This revised MacBook came with an aluminum case and a giant touch pad.

**↘ 2001, First iPod**
The iPod launched with a 1.5 in (4 cm) hard disk able to hold up to 1,000 tracks, but was compatible only with Apple computers.

**↑ 2007, iPhone**
Following years of speculation, Apple's first touch-screen-enabled smartphone went on sale. The 8 GB model cost $599.

**2010, iPhone 4**
Apple's fourth version of the iPhone featured a new steel and glass frame, and a new "retina" display, allowing ultra-sharp text and images.

**↘ 2009, iPod Touch**
Half-iPod and half-iPhone (but without voice calls), the iPod Touch has up to 64GB of internal storage.

**↘ 2003, Power Mac G5**
Eleven hundred of these high-performance machines were linked together to form the System X supercomputer cluster at Virginia Tech.

**↘ 2007, iMac**
Completely restyled iMacs with slim aluminum bodies were released in 20 in (50 cm) and 24 in (60 cm) screen versions.

**↘ 2009, Magic Mouse**
This wireless mouse was the first to feature multi-touch sensing (as used on the iPhone).

**↓ 2010, Apple TV**
This small device allowed users to stream video and music from iTunes, YouTube, and elsewhere.

**↓ 2000, G4 Cube**
unusual cube-shaped desktop [comp]uter with a clear acrylic outer the G4 Cube is still in demand for use as a fish tank or "Mac-quarium."

**↑ 2008, MacBook Air**
Just 0.2 in (4 mm) thick in places, with a body made from one sheet of aluminum, the Air was the first Apple to offer solid-state storage.

# What's behind a website?

A website is a collection of documents called web pages, which contain text, images, and links to other web pages. Most websites are created using a code called Hypertext Markup Language (HTML). There is software that sets up a website structure to which the user adds text and images.

## Language of the Web

HTML was developed by British Web pioneer Tim Berners-Lee and, with revisions, is still the most common way to format text and images to form a web page. HTML provides a wide range of coded commands, known as tags, that allow users to format text, insert photos, graphics, or multimedia files, and build tables of information. Links must also be established between the website's own pages.

## What else do you need?

Once you have a website you need a web hosting company to host it on a server, making it available 24/7. You also need an Internet connection to upload your pages to the server and a name. This consists of a top-level domain name after the dot (such as **.com**) and your website title.

## What is a blog?

The term "blog" comes from "web log"—a space online used like a diary or journal to post messages. It's easy to start a blog. They are often part of a regular website, and there are also dedicated blog hosts. All you have to do is sign up. Blogs are regularly updated and most are interactive, allowing visitors to leave comments.

## Browsers

A web browser is an application that gives you access to the Web. It translates HTML tags to display web pages on your computer. This laptop screen (right) displays a website's home page and the HTML code used to create it. For a website to reach as many people as possible, its pages must be compatible with all the most popular browers.

Finder   File   Edit   View   Go

Selecting "view source" in a browser reveals the HTML code

The web page's main content begins here

This code tells the website which image to display

Instructs the browser to open a new window

Images are hyperlinked to another web page

```
</HEAD>

<script language="ja
src="http://us.pengu
</script>

<script language="Ja
src="http://us.pengu
>

<body>

<!-- main content ar
<div id="container">
<!-- header -->
<div id="header"><h1
width="122" height="
</div>
<!-- end header -->
<p>Click on a flag t
<div class="clear"><

<!-- flags  -->
<!--flags row 1 -->
<div class="flagsect
uk.co.uk" onClick="n
uk.html'+redirectStr
src="images/uk_flag.
United Kingdom</a></
<div class="flagsect
onClick="newindow('c
usa.html'+redirectSt
src="images/us_flag.
United States</a></d

<div class="flagsect
onClick="newindow('c
canada.html'+redirec
src="images/ca_flag.
  Canada</a></div>
<div class="flagsect
onClick="newindow('c
australia.html'+redi
src="images/au_flag.
  Australia</a></div
<div class="flagsect
href="http://www.dor
onClick="newindow('c
germany.html'+redire
src="images/ge_flag.
  Germany</a></div>
```

//dk.com/

tic/misc/us/mainscript.js">

tic/misc/all/commonjs.js"></script

es/dk_logo.gif" alt="DK"
</h1>

h country</p>

ttp://www.dorlingkindersley-
', 'choose-
 false;"><img
ag" /><br />

ttp://us.penguingroup.com"

n false;"><img
ag" /><br />

ttp://cn.dk.com"

eturn false;"><img
ian flag" /><br />

ttp://www.penguin.com.au/dk"

);return false;"><img
alia flag" /><br />

erlag.de"

return false;"><img
n flag" /><br />

### Did you know?
By the end of 2010, there were an estimated 255 million websites worldwide. The number of individual web pages is in the trillions.

Website address, or domain name

Flags act as hyperlinks, (active links) taking you to a new web page

Dorling Kindersley – Illustrated Reference Publisher

http://www.dk.com →

Search engine

Dorling Kindersley

# DK www.dk.com

Click on a flag to visit a chosen country

**United Kingdom**  **United States**  **Canada**  **Australia**

**India**  **South Africa**  **China**  **Spain**

Firefox

Ps  Id  Br  Ai

# What do search engines do?

The Internet is beyond enormous. Billions of web pages, many of which are unhelpfully entitled "page 1" or "home," sit on web servers that also have technical or cryptic names and are impossible to find by yourself. Search engines cut through all of this complexity to provide you with a series of results to your requests for information. Their value and importance to Internet users has skyrocketed, turning the most successful into enormous businesses, handling vast amounts of data. In 1998, Google handled around 10,000 search queries per day. In 2010, that figure had risen to more than a billion.

## Baidu

Founded in 2000 by Robin Li and Eric Xu, Baidu is a Chinese-language search engine that continues to grow. Google spotted its potential in 2005 when it offered to buy it for $1.6 billion and was turned down. Baidu now indexes more than 740 million web pages and is responsible for 73 percent of the search requests made in China.

- Baidu makes its money from advertising, including a system where advertisers bid to get their ads and links placed alongside certain search results. It has proven successful—Baidu made a $599 million profit in 2010.

- "Search is a highly competitive game. For a user to leave us and go to somebody else, it's just one click." —Kaiser Kuo, Baidu spokesperson, 2010

---

What do search engines do? → Search engine

http://www.whatdosearchenginesdo.com →

What do search engines do? →

Web | Images | Videos | Maps | Shopping | Mail | More →

Ask  Google  Bing  Yahoo!  Baidu  AOL  Monster.com  TinEye  Seznam  Naver  News →

## Search engine

What do search engines do?

About 240,000,000 results | 0.10 seconds |

### Engine explosion

Before the World Wide Web, there were still search engines that looked for the names of files available over the Internet. One of the first, and best-known, is Archie, created by Canadian student Alam Emtage in 1990. The mid-to-late 1990s saw a battle between search's big beasts, including AltaVista, Lycos, Infoseek, Magellan, and Yahoo!, before Google rose to prominence.

Cached | Similar

**Everything**

Images
Videos
News
Shopping
Real-time
More

Web history | Settings → | Chat | Mail | Sign out

Search engine

Search

Advance search

## Archie Query Form

Search for

## Search Engine Share

Worldwide, Google dominates the search engine market to a spectacular extent. In January 2011, NetMarketShare reported that while Yahoo! had 6.14, Bing 3.68, and Baidu 2.92 percent of global market share, Google's search engines accounted for 85.37 percent. In a handful of countries, however, locally produced search engines still outrank Google. These include Naver in South Korea and Yandex in Russia, while in the Czech Republic, Google is locked in an ongoing battle with Seznam.cz to be number one.

When you type keywords into a search engine, your request is sent to the engine's index, which seeks out matches among its masses of data, orders them according to their rank (see below), and then returns a series of results pages. All of this happens in a fraction of a second.

Cached | Similar

## Web crawling

A search request accesses an enormous body of data stored on a search engine's index servers. These indexes are compiled using automated computer scripts called crawlers. These crawl through the entire World Wide Web, scouring web pages and sending back their results to the index.

Cached | Similar

## Search algorithms

The data in an index server is stored as a form of database. Each search engine uses a different method to search for a user's keyword using a set of search rules called an algorithm. These are highly complex and involve dozens or sometimes hundreds of different elements. Search algorithms tend to be closely guarded trade secrets.

Cached | Similar

## Ranking pages

No matter what algorithm is used, all search engines seek to rank web pages in order of their relevance to the search the user has requested. They do this by looking for the search keywords featured throughout each web page, but give greater weight to them when they occur in the title of the web page or in its headings. They also count the frequency with which the keyword appears on the page to assess how relevant the page is to the search.

Cached | Similar

## Search Engine Optimization (SEO)

There is fierce competition to make it to the front page of search results, especially in common subjects such as music or shopping that may already be populated by thousands of rival websites. SEO experts use a variety of techniques, including adjusting a web page's keywords and title, and fostering links to strong websites. Some also use "black hat techniques" — these frowned-upon methods include keyword stuffing (adding lots of popular keywords to a web page that aren't relevant) and link farms (where hundreds of websites all link to every other web page), trying to give them a boost in the rankings.

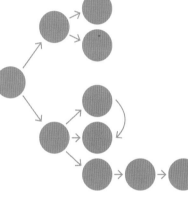

*"The ultimate search engine would basically understand everything in the world and it would always give you the right thing. And we're a long, long way from that."*
**Larry Page,** cofounder and CEO of Google

Web  Images  Videos  Maps  News  Shopping  Gmail  more ▼                    | iGoogle | Settings ▼ | Sign out

# Google

## Who invented Google?

Google Search          I'm feeling lucky

In 1995, 22-year-old Larry Page was shown around Stanford University by another student, Sergey Brin. The two disagreed on pretty much everything. However, the next year, when they ended up working together on a new search engine called BackRub, the two of them got along better. They also hit upon a winning formula that would soon become Google, the world's most popular search engine. In 2009, *Forbes* magazine described Page and Brin as the fifth-most-powerful people in the world.

## PageRank

Early search engines ranked web pages by how often the search term appeared on the page. Page and Brin's PageRank system used in Google went much further. It analyzed the number, quality, and importance of other pages that linked to the web page to produce more accurate and useful search results. Today, PageRank is just one of more than 200 different factors that enable most Google searches to be fast, accurate, and relevant.

**Sergey Brin →**
Sergey's father was a math professor and his mother was a space scientist. He was born in Moscow but left Russia for the United States at the age of six. Brin has donated more than $4 million to a space-tourism company.

**Larry Page →**
Larry's parents were both computer-science professors. While studying computer science himself at the University of Michigan, Page built an ink-jet plotter-printer out of Lego bricks. He and Brin co-own a Boeing 767 aircraft as well as two business jets.

## Growing fast

Brin and Page renamed BackRub "Google" in 1997 and the following year formed a company. At first, they operated out of a friend's garage in Menlo Park, California, but Google grew quickly. In 2000, Brin and Page released 10 foreign-language versions. In 2002, this grew to 72, one of which was in Klingon, the fictional language from *Star Trek*. By this time, Google's search index of more than a billion web pages made it the largest in the world.

**Reader →**

## Branching out

In order to stay ahead of rivals and attract valuable advertising, Google continued to add new features, including news, book, and image searches. Google Maps arrived in 2005, while Google Chrome is one of the top two web browsers in many countries. Not all Google's projects have been resounding successes. Google Answers, Google Lively (a 3-D virtual world), and Google Wave (a social networking site) didn't attract enough of a following and were shut down.

**YouTube →** You Tube

## The Googleplex

Google has offices in more than 50 locations, but its headquarters is in Mountain View, California. Long hours and hard work are part of Googleplex life, but there's plenty of fun to be had as well. There are weekly roller hockey matches in the parking lot, and the buildings also boast a gym, two swimming pools, pool tables, beach volleyball courts, a giant dinosaur skeleton, more than a dozen cafés, and even an adult-sized rubber-ball pit.

**Chrome ↑**

# "Don't be evil!"

*The informal motto of Google, which aims to be successful while always doing the right thing.*

**Blogger ↑**

**Google Earth →**

**Gmail ↑**

## 20-percent time

Google allows its employees to spend up to a fifth of their work week on special pet projects. Brin and Page believe that if an engineer is passionate about a project, it has the best chance of being a success. Google News, the Orkut social networking site, and Gmail, which has more than 146 million users, are three successful applications created by Google staff using 20-percent time.

**Images →**

## Google facts

● An estimated 80 to 85 percent of all queries on the Internet are typed into Google's search engines, and google.com is the most visited website in the world.

● According to ComScore in 2010, 34,000 searches are made on Google every second. That's about 88 billion searches a month.

● The first doodle (above) livened up Google's sparse home page in 1998. Now, an entire team is responsible for the Google doodles.

● Google makes its money from advertising, helping direct web users (traffic) to advertisers' websites. In 2009, advertisers paid Google $22.9 billion.

● Since 2001, Google has bought more than 80 companies, including YouTube, Blogger, photo-sharing site Picasa, and slide.com.

● In 1999, Brin and Page offered Google to a rival company, Excite, for just $1 million. Excite turned down the offer.

● Google strives to be eco-friendly. Solar panels generate up to 30 percent of the Googleplex's electricity and, each year, goats are brought in to "mow" the grass.

● Brin and Page pay themselves just a dollar a year—but their Google shares make them billionaires.

● "Google" is a play on *googol*, which means 1 followed by 100 zeroes.

# Server farm

A server is a computer that handles files, tasks, and data from other computers, known as clients. A server farm is a collection of computer servers in one location. Server farms can perform a wide range of tasks, from storing companies' computer data securely to hosting websites and transmitting data over the Internet. Large quantities of data can flow to and from the server farm and the businesses and organizations that are its customers.

**The Pionen facility**
In 2007 and 2008, more than 140,000 cu ft (4,000 cu m) of solid rock were blasted away to turn this former nuclear bunker into a server farm. It covers an area of 12,000 sq ft (1,110 sq m).

Office

Kitchen

Ventilation room

Machine room

Servers

Conference room

Cooling equipment

Backup power

## Super server

About 100 ft (30 m) below the city of Stockholm is a bunker hewn out of granite rock. The Pionen data center belongs to Bahnhof, one of Sweden's biggest Internet service providers. Secured behind its 16 in (40 cm) thick steel doors, more than 6,000 computer servers shift millions of bytes of data over computer networks.

## World apart

The Pionen data center features lamps that simulate daylight, large numbers of plants, artificial waterfalls, and a giant 570-gallon (2,600-liter) saltwater fish tank. The floor of its conference room is a replica of the Moon's surface.

## Cooling issues

Electricity is one of a server farm's biggest expenses. It is needed both to power the machines and to keep them cool. At the Pionen data center, two giant diesel engines from a German submarine power the generators (pictured) that provide backup electricity. The server farm has a warning system in case there is a security breach or a major technical fault with a group of servers. This consists of loud horns from the same submarine.

# Our time online

People spend their time online in a vast number of different ways. Some use their time to learn about a subject in depth while others prefer skimming through many different topics, picking up snippets and facts along the way. Many people get involved in online communities dedicated to particular hobbies or interests, from supporting the same sports team to sharing their passion for vintage cars or photography, or their experiences of owning a pet. Whatever their interests, most people tend to use the Internet for many different purposes throughout a single day.

**Really Simple Syndication (RSS)**
It wasn't that long ago that the only way to keep track of updates on your favorite website was to find it in your web browser, again and again. RSS or Really Simple Syndication automates the process for you by sending headlines and summaries of updates and new content from websites you subscribe to. New material is sent out to you automatically as it is posted online.

## Morning news

Grabbing the morning news used to be a simple matter of waiting for the newspaper to be delivered or switching on the radio. Now, many cannot resist starting the day by powering up their laptop or PC to read the latest headlines online. Some head directly to a particular news agency or media site while others use RSS feeds (see above right).

## Off to work

Millions of people take long journeys on public transportation to and from work. These commuters are well-served by technologies designed for use on the move, from media players with headphones that cancel out much of the background noise, to smartphones capable of picking up e-mails or displaying web pages.

## Checking the inbox

Many people start their work day by checking their e-mail inbox, whether they are traveling, in the office, or working from home. An estimated 2.8 million e-mails are sent every second by the world's 1.9 billion e-mail users, many of whom have more than one account. E-mail numbers are increased further by junk messages known as spam.

### cafe

## Social networking

Keeping in touch with friends through jokes, banter, and games, finding old friends, and making new ones are part of the appeal of social networking sites such as Facebook, MySpace, and Bebo. Still growing in popularity, new apps, games, and quizzes, especially on Facebook, are causing people to spend more and more time on these sites.

## Working from home

Many people now work for companies from home, accessing company information and contacting coworkers via an Internet connection. The Internet has helped thousands of people start their own businesses, getting advice, contacts, and even funding from online sources, and getting orders and work via their websites.

## Blogging

Lots of people like to share their opinions with others online. Newspaper and other media websites encourage readers' comments since they help keep people on their sites for longer and generate additional content for free. Blogs contain a person's thoughts, views, and stories as well as links to other blogs or websites.

## Money matters

More and more people handle their personal finances online, enjoying the convenience of online banking and trusting in the security layers and encryption software employed by banks to protect their accounts. Others invest via online stock trading, while financial news updates allow people to keep track of financial markets all over the world.

## Shop 'til you drop

E-commerce has proved very popular with customers, who are able to find and buy goods from all over the world via international shopping sites. Shoppers take advantage of price-comparison websites to find the best price, scour the net for discount coupons, and may not buy until they've read online reviews of products.

## Face to face

A webcam, either built into or attached to a monitor or laptop screen, allows images to be sent and received, keeping people in touch, face-to-face. Video conferencing means a meeting can be held in different locations at the same time, while video relay services enable people to communicate with sign language over the Internet through an interpreter.

## Face the facts

Up-to-the-minute access to facts, scores, and updates has become essential for many, now equipped with easy-to-use web searches by voice on some smartphones or by keyword on e-readers, tablets, and PCs. Celebrity gossip websites and sports update services that offer results and news are particularly popular.

## Evening entertainment

An evening in with the laptop might involve a mixture of e-mails, social networking, and catching up on TV shows using video sites like Hulu, on which Americans watch 924 million videos per month, or YouTube, which has 12.2 billion video clips viewed every month. You can also access movie-streaming websites and download music.

## Late-night gaming

Gaming is popular at all hours with many Internet users, who enjoy the range of highly addictive games available online. The evening is often a good time for more involved gaming, for competing with players around the world, or for using forums to share and swap tips and tricks, including cheats or games.

# Social networking

Keeping in touch with friends, known as social networking, now occupies more of people's time online than any other activity. Statistics for June 2010 saw social networking sites such as Bebo, MySpace, and Facebook account for 22.7 percent of all time spent on the Web in the United States. In contrast, Americans spend 10.2 percent of their time on online games, 8.3 percent on e-mails, and 3.9 percent watching videos.

## Facebook facts

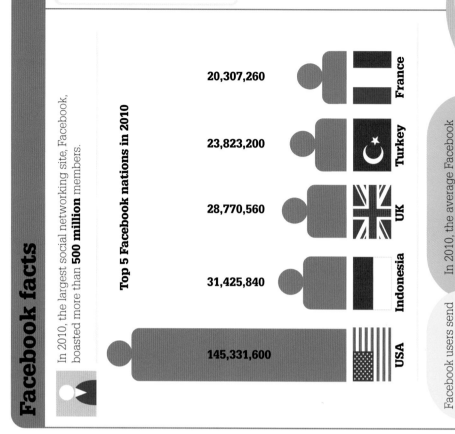

In 2010, the largest social networking site, Facebook, boasted more than **500 million** members.

### Top 5 Facebook nations in 2010

| USA | Indonesia | UK | Turkey | France |
|---|---|---|---|---|
| 145,331,600 | 31,425,840 | 28,770,560 | 23,823,200 | 20,307,260 |

Facebook users send **4 billion** messages every day.

In 2010, the average Facebook user created **90** pieces of content every month, from uploaded photos to messages.

Thanks to around **300,000** Facebook users who helped provide translations, Facebook is now available in 70 different languages including

## Networking nations

According to one survey, in 2010 the nations with the highest percentage of Internet users active on at least one social networking site were:

Brazil – **95%**

USA – **84%**

Portugal – **82%**

## BOOM!

Globally, there was an **82.2%** increase in the time spent on social networking sites between December 2008 and December 2009.

## Turn it off!

According to a 2010 study, **48%** of social networkers confessed that they update or check Twitter or Facebook after having gone to bed or first thing in the morning.

## Silver surfers

Social networking was once thought to be only a young person's game. Now, everyone is getting in on the act. In early 2010, statistics showed that **47% of 50 to 64-year-old Internet users** surf social networking sites. And **26%** of Internet users **over 60** use it to social network.

## Watch the time

The average visitor to a social network site spent **66%** more time on such sites in 2010 than they did a year earlier.

English is the most popular language on Facebook, with **213.2 million** users —**52.2%** of total users. Next is Spanish **(61.2 million)**, French **(23.5 million)**, Turkish **(21.9 million)**, and Indonesian **(20.5 million)**.

Facebook continues to grow rapidly. In October 2010 alone, an additional **2,974,000** Indonesians joined up, along with **1.66 million** Mexicans, and **1.56 million** new users from India.

Every month, around **290 million** Facebook users log on just to play games.

The majority of Facebook gamers—a surprising **69%**—are women.

With more than **75 million** registered players, *FarmVille* is the biggest Facebook game of all. Players plant, tend, and harvest virtual crops.

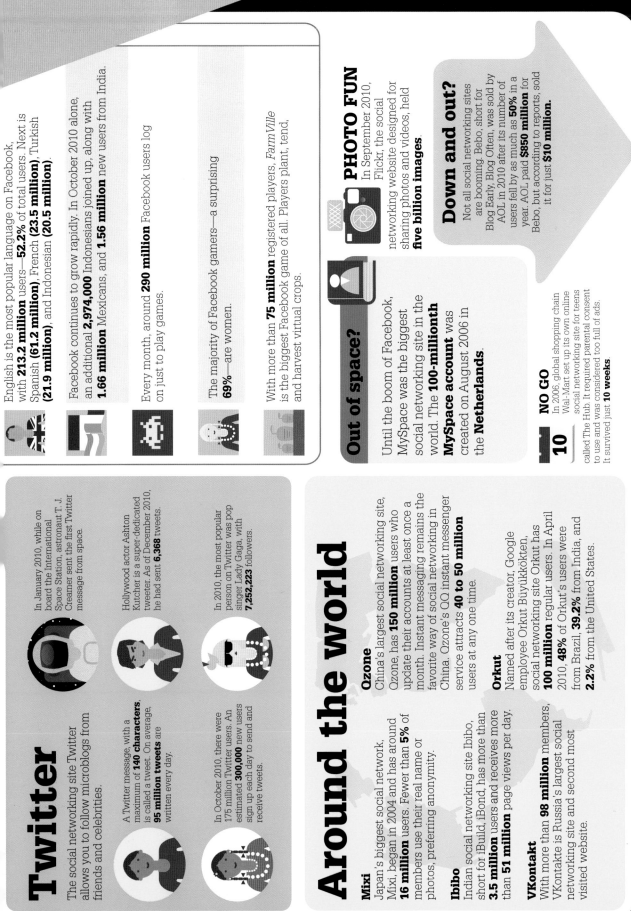

# Twitter

The social networking site Twitter allows you to follow microblogs from friends and celebrities.

A Twitter message, with a maximum of **140 characters**, is called a tweet. On average, **95 million tweets** are written every day.

In October 2010, there were 175 million Twitter users. An estimated **300,000** new users sign up each day to send and receive tweets.

In January 2010, while on board the International Space Station, astronaut T. J. Creamer sent the first Twitter message from space.

Hollywood actor Ashton Kutcher is a super-dedicated tweeter. As of December 2010, he had sent **6,368** tweets.

In 2010, the most popular person on Twitter was pop singer Lady Gaga, with **7,252,223** followers.

# Around the world

### Mixi
Japan's biggest social network, Mixi, began in 2004 and has around **16 million** users. Fewer than **5%** of members use their real name or photos, preferring anonymity.

### Ibibo
Indian social networking site Ibibo, short for iBuild, iBond, has more than **3.5 million** users and receives more than **51 million** page views per day.

### VKontakt
With more than **98 million** members, VKontakte is Russia's largest social networking site and second most visited website.

### Qzone
China's largest social networking site, Qzone, has **150 million** users who update their accounts at least once a month. Instant messaging remains the favorite way of social networking in China. Qzone's QQ instant messenger service attracts **40 to 50 million** users at any one time.

### Orkut
Named after its creator, Google employee Orkut Buyukkokten, social networking site Orkut has **100 million** regular users. In April 2010, **48%** of Orkut's users were from Brazil, **39.2%** from India, and **2.2%** from the United States.

## Out of space?

Until the boom of Facebook, MySpace was the biggest social networking site in the world. The **100-millionth MySpace account** was created on August 2006 in the **Netherlands**.

## PHOTO FUN

In September 2010, Flickr, the social networking website designed for sharing photos and videos, held **five billion images**.

## Down and out?

Not all social networking sites are booming. Bebo, short for Blog Early, Blog Often, was sold by AOL in 2010 after its number of users fell by as much as **50%** in a year. AOL paid **$850 million** for Bebo, but according to reports, sold it for just **$10 million**.

## NO GO

**10**

In 2006, global shopping chain Wal-Mart set up its own online social networking site for teens called The Hub. It required parental consent to use and was considered too full of ads. It survived just **10 weeks**.

"Once every 100 years, media changes. The last 100 years have been defined by the mass media. In the next 100 years, information won't be just pushed out to people: It will be shared among the millions of connections people have."

## *Mark Zuckerberg*

*Mark Zuckerberg (born 1984) is the originator of social networking monster Facebook. The site grew out of Facemash, which allowed students at Harvard University to rate pictures of each other. Zuckerberg and three friends launched Facebook from their dorm rooms in 2004, and had a million users within 10 months. The story of Facebook's creation was the subject of a movie,* The Social Network *(2010). Zuckerberg still runs Facebook and is said to have turned down takeover offers from Yahoo!, Viacom, and Microsoft among others. In January 2011, Facebook was valued at more than $50 billion.*

### Did you know?

The styling of Facebook's website is predominantly blue. This is because Zuckerberg has red-green color blindness and sees the color blue best.

# The growth of the Web

The World Wide Web is exploding in size. From a barely noticeable handful of websites 20 years ago, it has mushroomed into a gigantic resource. In 2010 alone, around 21.4 million new websites were added to the Web. And as huge countries like China, India, Indonesia, and Brazil get more and more of their population online, it's only set to get bigger and bigger.

North America
266,224,500
**77.4%**

Europe
475,069,448
**58.4%**

Asia
825,094,396
**21.5%**

Middle East
63,240,946
**29.8%**

Africa
110,931,700
**10.9%**

Latin America/Caribbean
204,689,836
**34.5%**

Oceania / Australia
21,272,470
**61.3%**

↑ **World statistics**
The Internet has not penetrated evenly across the world. The figures above show first the number of Internet users in each region in 2010, and then give this as a percentage of the total population.

## Number of websites

| 1993 | 1994 | 1995 | 1996 | 2009 |
|------|------|------|------|------|
| 130 | 2,738 | 23,500 | 230,000 | 215,675,903 |

The number of individual web pages now numbers in the trillions.

## Number of worldwide Internet users

| 2000 | 2010 |
|------|------|
| 360,985,492 | 1,966,514,816 |

That's a growth of
**448.8%**

In 2010, the global percentage of people with Internet access was 28.7%.

# Countries with the most Internet users:

China 420,000,000

USA 239,893,600

Japan 99,143,700

India 81,000,000

Brazil 75,943,600

## The name game
The domain name of a website (the letters after the dot at the end of the address) tell you a lot about it—for example, whether it is a government (**.gov**) or educational (**.edu**) organization, or the country of the website's origin (**.fr** for France).

- The tiny Pacific island nation of Tuvalu (population 11,600) received a windfall from 2000 onward when it sold the rights to its **.tv** domain names, particularly to TV channels.

- Two other countries with domains sought after by radio stations are: **.fm** - Federated states of Micronesia **.am** - Armenia

## What are we doing?
Below are the top activities we engage in online, the percentage of daily users, and the average amount of time they spend on the activity per week.

**E-mail**
72% of users send e-mail
4.4 hours average per week

**News**
55% check news
2.7 hours average per week

**Social**
46% social network
4.6 hours average per week

**Interest**
46% pursue interests online
3.9 hours average per week

**Knowledge**
39% look up information
3.1 hours average per week

**Multimedia**
37% watch films or TV
3.7 hours average per week

**Gaming**
27% play games
2.9 hours average per week

**Browsing**
24% browse generally
2.3 hours average per week

**Admin**
21% do personal admin
1.7 hours spent per week

**Organize**
19% plan their lives online
1.6 hours average per week

**Shopping**
12% shop online
1.8 hours average per week

## Most visited websites
Google publishes a list of the number of monthly unique visitors the world's other most popular websites receive. While the exact number remains a mystery for Google itself, it's safe to assume that it would top this list.

facebook 590,000,000

You Tube 490,000,000

YAHOO! UK 450,000,000

Windows Live 340,000,000

WIKIPEDIA 310,000,000

## Top languages used on the Web

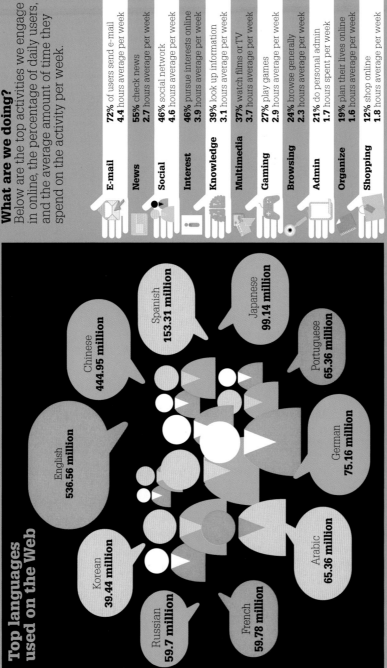

English 536.56 million

Chinese 444.95 million

Spanish 153.31 million

Japanese 99.14 million

Portuguese 65.36 million

German 75.16 million

Arabic 65.36 million

French 59.78 million

Russian 59.7 million

Korean 39.44 million

## Haves and have nots
There's a big difference between the populations of developed nations with access to the Internet and those of developing nations.

Developed nations **71%**

Developing nations **21%**

The top three countries in terms of the percentage of their populations with Internet access are:

Iceland **97.6%**

Norway **94.9%**

Sweden **92.5%**

The countries with the lowest rate of Internet access are:

Myanmar **0.2%**

East Timor **0.1%**

# Access all areas

Imagine facing a 2-day trek every time you wanted to check your e-mail. That's the prospect facing many who live in rural parts of mountainous Nepal. Here, on the "Roof of the World," fewer than three percent of the country's 29 million people have direct Internet access. Nepal is far from alone. There is a huge digital divide between the Internet haves and have-nots around the world. All kinds of initiatives, both big and small, are working to shrink the gap.

### Mahabir Pun

Returning home to Nepal after studying in the United States, Mahabir Pun created a wireless connection between his village and its neighbors in 2001, using an old TV satellite dish. Since then, Pun has helped bring Internet access to more than 100 Nepalese villages, using donated PCs and parts.

### Did you know?

According to Internet World Stats in 2010, more than three-quarters of the U.S. population were Internet users. By contrast, just 0.3 percent of the population of the African nation of Sierra Leone used the Internet.

## Network Nepal

Many communities in rural Nepal are remote, at high altitude, cut off by steep valleys, and poorly served by roads or electricity. Building long-distance Wi-Fi networks in this terrain has been a huge challenge. Materials have been carried up by hand to construct the relay towers that beam the signals through the narrow valleys. The highest tower stands 11,800 ft (3,600 m) above sea level and is manned by a yak farmer, who must check the connections every day.

## Online impact

The Internet has brought together isolated Nepalese communities. School children work online, farmers can buy and sell on a local trading website, and health workers use webcams so patients can be examined by hospital doctors in the capital, Kathmandu.

## Everest 3G

In 2010, the Nepalese telecom company Ncell brought wireless 3G Internet and phone coverage to Mount Everest—its climbers, guides, and nearby villages. Since there is no electricity supply, the system's 10 base stations are powered by solar panels, with batteries for backup. The highest of the stations is 17,060 ft (5,200 m) above sea level.

# How the Web is run

The World Wide Web is huge and complex, so who runs it all? Surely, someone must be in charge? It's not the Internet service providers (ISPs) who connect you to the Internet, or the telecom companies who supply phone lines and infrastructure. Nor is it national governments or the UN. The answer is that no single organization administers all websites and the content that flows between them.

## Did you know?

Lurking beyond the Web that is accessible to search engines lies the "deep web," millions of private pages and information held in databases that search engines cannot reach.

## Government interference

Search engines receive requests from national governments asking for the removal of material from their search results or, in Google's case, from either their search results or other Google products such as YouTube or Google Groups. In the first six months of 2010, Google received more than 5,000 requests from the U.S. government for material to be removed or for information on users of Google products.

## How big is the Web?

For a system that is all about information on any topic imaginable, from aardvarks to zip codes, it's surprising how little definitive data there is on the Web and its size. This is in part due to its constant growth and changing nature. A survey in January 2011 counted 273,301,445 websites. These generate more than 14 billion web pages.

### Task force

The Internet Engineering Task Force (IETF) is an international, open community of network engineers, companies, and researchers who try to keep networks running smoothly while improving Internet standards.

### W3C

Formed and led by Tim Berners-Lee, the World Wide Web Consortium (W3C) looks after the standards that underpin websites and web pages.

## National restrictions

The World Wide Web's pioneers envisioned an open, free flow of information throughout the world, but national governments sometimes don't let that happen. Some websites that are accepted in one country may break the laws of another and are blocked or banned.

### Italy

Since 2006, gambling on foreign websites has been illegal in Italy. Gambling, betting, and bookmaking websites from abroad are blocked.

### North Africa

During unrest in north Africa in 2011, the Twitter website was blocked in both Tunisia and Egypt to prevent it from being used to organize protests.

## Many helpers

There may be no one in charge of the Web, but don't panic. Many organizations are involved in maintaining, managing, and planning different facets of the Internet. These include international working parties that ensure that web technology works in all languages, scripts, and cultures—an enormous task.

### Internet Society

Formed in 1992, the Internet Society is a nonprofit organization that has more than 44,000 members and tries to plan and campaign to avoid future problems with Internet growth.

> "The Internet is not a thing, a place, a single technology, or a mode of governance. It is an agreement."
>
> **John Gage,** Director of Science, Sun Microsystems, Inc.

## Internet to splinternet?

The Internet has relied on agreement between many parties to survive and prosper worldwide. Could a lack of future agreement, censorship, and other restrictions placed on websites by national governments lead to a "splinternet," with different standards in different nations? No one is certain, but changes are likely as more and more of the four billion people currently without access get online.

## Walled gardens?

In the early days of the Web, major ISPs such as Compuserve and America OnLine (AOL) walled off their content, only allowing access to paying, registered users. After years of offering free content and services on the Web, many companies, including the *New York Times*, are returning to this model and charging for access in an attempt to recoup the vast costs of their websites.

## Net neutrality

There are other threats besides government interference that challenge the ability of the Internet to deliver all data equally to everyone, a principle known as network neutrality. Some ISPs and companies want to create a "fast lane" on the Internet that can be used by customers who pay more for websites and data. Those who support neutrality fear that this would lead to unequal and unfair service.

## Political censorship

Some countries block websites that criticize the government or country, or provide details on sensitive subjects such as anti-government protests and marches. In nations such as Cuba and Myanmar, with very low private Internet access, government-run cybercafes and access points may be heavily censored, with thousands of websites banned.

### South Korea
South Koreans visiting websites with more than 100,000 members have to register with their real name and national identity card number.

## Leaky bucket

Attempts to censor or remove material from the Internet are not always successful—it's sometimes described as a leaky bucket, because it's so easy to copy and redistribute information. Attempts at censorship can generate great international interest, and mirror sites that are copies of the original site often spring up, hosted in other countries.

### Turkey
After its founder, Mustafa Kemal Atatürk, was mocked in YouTube videos, Turkey banned the website in the country for two years.

### Georgia
In 2008, during the war with Russia over the region of South Ossetia, the government of Georgia banned all websites that ended in .ru, originating from Russia.

# The good side of the Web

The founders of the World Wide Web made it freely available because they thought it could be a powerful force for good. In many ways, they were right. In its relatively short life so far, the World Wide Web has been an astonishing success, helping to inform and transform millions of lives. It provides a platform for new businesses, puts people with shared interests in touch, and provides a convenient, regularly updated source of news and entertainment for millions every day.

## Free software

The Web holds a growing collection of computer programs that are free for anyone with Internet access to download. People often take these resources for granted, but it is quite remarkable that the results of thousands of hours of hard work are given away. The two main kinds of free software are freeware and open-source programs. Freeware is software that is free for personal or non-commercial use. Open-source programs go even further, offering the entire program code and background details so that fellow software designers can alter or improve the program.

## Wayback Machine

Interested in time travel? The Wayback Machine is a gigantic archive of web pages dating back to 1996. Users can see what a website's content was like at different points in the past—for free. In 2007, the California-based organization performed a massive web crawl in order to take a global snapshot of the World Wide Web. It cataloged and archived two billion web pages. Archives like this will be invaluable to future Internet historians.

## Sharing expertise

The Web is bursting with knowledge on a vast range of subjects. Experts and enthusiasts give up their time to offer insights and information on personal websites or take part in collaborative projects such as iFixit, which offers repair manuals for hundreds of electrical devices. Surfers can download sports rules and coaching tips from governing bodies, identify wildlife they have spotted, learn a language, or get advice on how to improve their paintings, photography, or music, all for free.

### Did you know?

On December 10, 2010, Freerice.com users donated more than 60 million grains of rice to starving people worldwide. All they had to do was click on advertisers' links on websites.

## Helping others

Charities and campaign groups use the Web to raise awareness of issues. Their websites feature facts and figures, video case studies, and interviews. Many provide helpful free resources, such as advice on how to deal with bullying, eating disorders, alcohol, drugs, or gang violence. Charities can raise funds by running online campaigns or organizing virtual volunteering, in which people donate their time or skills over the Internet to help a cause some distance away.

## Freecycle

In 2003, recycling activist Deron Beal sent out an email to about 40 friends and local charities around Tucson, Arizona. He wanted to set up a system in which people offered unwanted goods to others rather than throw them away. The Freecycle Network now operates in more than 85 countries and has more than seven million members. Its online notice boards advertise all kinds of gifted items, from baby carriages to printers.

### Did you know?

Michelle Miles, a 19-year-old from Arkansas, began a charitable cause on Facebook. Her "Race to End Cancer" has more than six million members and has raised more than $80,000.

# The bad side of the Web

Most people build web pages in order to educate, inform, or entertain. Some, however, misuse the fabulous resource at their fingertips, and play pranks, start rumors, or build websites full of lies. Some use the Web, email, and instant messages to upset and intimidate people. Others spread malicious computer code that can damage computers or steal passwords, allowing criminals to divert money from victims' bank accounts.

## Viruses and worms

Computer viruses are types of malware that make copies of themselves and run automatically on a computer, often destroying files or even erasing hard disks. When a file containing a virus is sent to another computer, it can become infected, too. Worms are viruses that use network connections to spread automatically. Identified in 2008, the Conficker worm has infected millions of machines, including computers in the French navy and British police. It may have caused more than $9.5 billion of damage.

## Offensive sites

Many websites display images or discuss subjects, such as violence or sexual content, that are unsuitable for children and distasteful to many adults. Internet filters, such as Net Nanny, Safe Eyes, and Google's SafeSearch, can prevent these sites from being viewed by people who do not want to or should not see them.

## Did you know?

In 2009, 11 people in China were found guilty of using Trojans and other malware. They had stolen more than five million user names and passwords

## Malware

Computer software that is sent to your computer with mischievous or criminal intent is called malware. It includes viruses, worms, Trojans, and spyware. Malware can be just a harmless, if irritating, prank or designed for more serious purposes, such as stealing credit card and bank account details or crippling a victim's computer. Malware is a massive problem, with around 60,000 new malware threats identified every day.

## Phishing

Fake emails that seem to be from trusted sources, such as banks and Internet service providers, and ask you to update or verify your personal details, are examples of phishing. What are they hoping to catch? People's banking information and other personal details, which they can sell to other criminals or use directly to make purchases.

## Spam

In 2004, Bill Gates predicted that unsolicited bulk email (spam) would be stopped within 2 years. He was wrong. Despite the use of spam filters, junk emails still cram many people's inboxes. Most spam is sent out by zombies, PCs unknowingly infected with a virus or similar piece of malware that allows spammers to control them.

## Trojans and backdoors

Trojan horse programs masquerade as legitimate software, such as a free game or virus scanner, to trick users into running them. Once installed, they can introduce additional malware. Some Trojans install a backdoor—software that bypasses the computer's normal security to allow access to the entire machine. American hacker Albert Gonzalez used backdoor programs to steal details for as many as 170 million ATM and credit cards. In 2010, he was sentenced to 20 years in prison.

## Cyber-bullying

Bullying is very upsetting both face-to-face and online. Cyber-bullying can involve a victim being ridiculed, harassed, unfairly excluded from a forum or online game, or repeatedly locked out of their social network accounts. Cyber-bullies may bombard their victim's phone or computer with threatening texts, emails, and instant messages, or send them spam and malware. Some cyber-bullies pretend to be the victim online, wreaking havoc with the victim's life.

## Fiction, not fact

Errors, pranks, and lies can spread, given credibility by appearing on a website. The dhmo.org website warns people of a dangerous liquid, dihydrogen monoxide. Seven million people have visited the site and calls for DHMO to be banned have been made by politicians in New Zealand and the United States—but DHMO is just another name for water!

# Keeping us safe

Attempts at computer fraud and other crimes are an unpleasant fact of digital life. In their efforts to ward off attacks, police, software makers, and others involved with computer security give warnings of possible threats and come up with ways to keep computers and their users safe.

## Be aware

The first and best line of defense against computer threats is to be a careful user. Keep antivirus software and other security patches up-to-date. You should also never open suspicious e-mail attachments or reveal personal details online, and avoid counterfeit software and other illegal downloads.

## Did you know?

In 2010, PandaLabs, the virus research network, estimated that 57,000 fake websites open every week. They mimic more famous sites, such as eBay, Amazon, and PayPal, in an attempt to steal money.

## Scams

Many scam websites or e-mails offer famous brands at low prices. People pay but never receive their goods. In 2009, London's e-crime unit closed down more than 1,200 fraudulent shopping sites. Fake charity sites, made to resemble real appeals, are another scam.

## Password protection?

Hard-to-guess passwords off some protection. Unfortunate many people use the same w password for all their accoun Cyber-criminals can discover passwords with software tha through every possible chara combination. Longer passwo containing symbols and num take longer to crack.

## Top 10 wea passwords

1. password
2. 123456
3. qwerty
4. abc123
5. letmein
6. monkey
7. myspace1
8. password1
9. blink182
10. (your first name)

# Firewalls

A firewall is hardware or, more commonly, software that sits between your computer and the Internet or another network. Its preferences can be set to only let through certain actions, Internet addresses, or data. A firewall can prevent some viruses and hackers from gaining control of your computer, but it is safest to install antivirus software as well.

## Did you know?

Malware attacks can be literally out of this world. In 2008, a laptop taken to the International Space Station was found to be infected by the *Gammima.AG* worm, which steals passwords.

# Antivirus software

Antivirus programs are designed to scan your computer for signs of suspicious activity, seek out infected files, and check for files that match the profile of known malware. If the software discovers a suspicious file, it will offer a range of actions—deleting the file, trying to clean it, or disabling the file and housing it in a quarantine area or virus vault. Antivirus makers work overtime to develop successful fixes to existing malware, and to identify and repel new threats, which appear regularly.

# Cyber-cops

All around the world, governments, police, and intelligence forces are working hard to counter cyber-crime. As these crimes often cross borders, fighting them involves international collaboration. Investigators are becoming highly skilled at tracing suspicious activity, tracking Internet addresses, and uncovering the identities of anonymous cyber-criminals.

### The spam sender

McColo was a U.S.-based ISP that turned out to host a number of infamous botnets—computer programs that send out junk mail and malware—including Rustock, Storm, and Mega-D. After McColo was shut down in 2008, global spam quantities plummeted by between 40 and 75 percent.

### The virus writer

Masato Nakasuji was arrested in 2008 for writing the Harada virus, which replaced files with an image from a famous Japanese comic book series. Two years later, his Ika-tako virus infected at least 20,000 computers, replacing files with manga-style pictures of squid and octopuses he had drawn.

### The undercover agent

DarkMarket was an Internet forum where cyber-criminals could sell credit-card-copying machines and stolen data. What users didn't know was that Master Splyntr, the forum's administrator from 2006 to 2008, was actually an FBI agent, Keith Mularski. His undercover operation resulted in 56 arrests.

### The teenage hacker

In 2000, working under the alias MafiaBoy, 15-year-old Michael Calce from Canada hacked into the world's leading search engine, Yahoo!, and shut it down for an hour. He followed with attacks on the American news company CNN, eBay, and computer manufacturer Dell. He was caught after boasting about his exploits in Internet chat rooms.

## Online advertising

Many websites sell no goods or services at all but instead offer useful or interesting content free to their visitors. These sites are financed by advertising. The fees agreed for every 1,000 clicks on an ad or every 10,000 times it is viewed are tiny, but multiplied by millions of potential visitors they can result in big monthly fees.

### free download!

### Banner ads
A banner ad is a graphical bar or button usually located at the top or side of a website containing text and/or images. Clicking on it will often take you to the advertiser's web pages.

### In-betweeners
Interstitials are pages that appear during a delay that occurs between clicking on a Web link and the expected web page's appearance. They are often used by a website's sponsor or sold to other companies to advertise on.

### Tailored text ads
Text ads are becoming more sophisticated. Within a website, text ads can relate to the content of individual pages. If a user is viewing a page about skiing, for example, it might carry ads for ski gear or hotels at leading ski resorts.

### Before you go... did you know?

### Rich-media ads
Some ads try to grab your attention with fun multimedia elements such as sound, a video clip, or animation, including mini games to play.

### Sponsorships
Some websites are funded by a sponsor—in return, websites display the sponsor's logo or message prominently. The sponsor's logo is usually clickable, which means that clicking on it takes users to the sponsor's own website.

### Pesky pop-ups
Pop-up ads do just that—pop up on the page that a person is using. Starting out as a novelty, pop-ups have become an annoyance. Often, browsers and security software offer the option of blocking them.

### Brought to you by...

# Making money online

Running a personal website that has a few, simple pages can be free or cost a few pennies a week, depending on the Internet Service Provider. Larger websites are far more expensive. The costs for web design of the pages, professional hosting, search engine optimization, and regular content updates soon run into the thousands. So how do websites make back this money and then go on to earn a healthy profit?

### Did you know?
Web advertising is big business. From January to June 2010, American advertisers spent around $12.6 billion on online marketing.

## Freemium

An increasingly popular online business technique, a freemium offers basic access or a scaled-down version of a service for free. The hope is that enough users will choose to upgrade to a premium, paid-for service that offers more content or features. It is used by the Spotify music-streaming service, Skype, and YouSendIt, for example. On a similar model, some online games are free to play but charge for in-game items and upgrades, such as weapons or skills.

## Buyouts

Some companies offer such a strong product or have so many visitors to their website that bigger companies make a takeover offer or buyout. There are even websites that specialize in buying and selling websites, such as Flippa. The sums are usually small but occasionally a big buyout occurs. In 2007, for example, Yahoo! bought the Web e-mail company Zimbra for a cool $350 million.

## Did you know?

English schoolboy Tom Hadfield started posting soccer results in 1994 and began Soccernet the following year. In 1999, the website sold for $40 million.

## Big winner

In 2004, 14-year-old Ashley Qualls started her own website offering free graphics, templates, and tips on how to use them on MySpace. She paid eight dollars for the domain name whateverlife.com, but was soon receiving monthly checks from advertisers for up to $70,000. MySpace offered Qualls $1.5 million plus her choice of car for the site. She declined and, in 2009, relaunched it as a social networking site, WhateverLife 2.0.

## Sites without ads

Some companies' websites are not designed to turn a profit—they are part of a company's marketing budget and their job is simply to project a positive image of the company. Other websites raise money by selling products directly, such as merchandise or digital downloads. Some websites, from small charities to Wikipedia, rely on donations from individuals and companies to cover their costs.

## Million dollar homepage

In 2005, British student Alex Tew came up with an ingenious way to pay for his college education. He built a website of one million pixels and sold off blocks at a dollar per pixel to advertising banners. The website was filled in just five months and included a banner advertising Jack Black's rock group Tenacious D and another for the London *Times* newspaper. The last 1,000 pixels were auctioned on eBay for $38,100!

## Did you know?

Fashion sales website Boo.com went bust in 2000, having run up costs of about $200 million. Its spending included flying a top hairstylist from New York to London to style the virtual hair of the website's avatar, Miss Boo.

# E-buying and selling

E-commerce is business performed using electronic systems. It's mostly buying and selling over the Internet or other computer networks and it has grown from a tiny pinprick of activity in the 1970s to a massive industry. In China alone in 2010, an estimated $340 billion changed hands in e-commerce transactions. And it's only going to get bigger and bigger…

## eBay

Popular online auction site **eBay** started life as AuctionWeb, created by Pierre Omidyar in California in 1995. The first item ever sold was a broken laser pointer that went for $14.83.

### eBay best-sellers (by frequency)

**Every 3 seconds:** a woman's handbag
**Every 9 seconds:** a CD
**Every 21 seconds:** a mobile phone
**Every 120 seconds:** a soccer shirt

**90 million**

eBay has around **90 million** users, spending more than **$57 billion** each year.

### You can find anything on eBay…

In 2004, a **50,000-year-old mammoth** weighing 550,000 lb (250,000 kg), was sold for $98,000.

A **stain on the floor of a garage** that looked like a picture of Jesus was sold on eBay for $1,525.69.

In 2006, a **single Brussels sprout** left over from Christmas dinner fetched **$2,490** in an eBay auction. The seller, Leigh Knight of Stockton, England, donated the money to cancer research.

**Looking good**
A piece of jewelry sells every **4 minutes** on eBay India, where it is the most popular category of item for sale.

## amazon.com

Amazon, the world's largest online retailer, started out in the United States in 1995 as an online bookstore, but now sells almost everything. In 2009, it enjoyed total sales of **$24.51 billion.**

Amazon has **28,300 employees** worldwide.

### SHOPPING FRENZY
On December 15, 2008, **6.3 million** items were ordered on Amazon. That's 72.9 every second.

## craigslist

The online classified-ad site craigslist is one of the most visited websites in the world, and receives **20 billion** page views every month.

**1 million**
• The number of new job listings each month on craigslist.

Every month, **50 million** new ads are placed on craigslist.

The cost to place an ad? Free!

### BIG BUYS

eBay bought PayPal for **$1.5 billion** in 2002. It has bought up more than 20 other companies including Skype and Shopping.com.

In 2009, Amazon paid **$1.2 billion** to buy the online clothing-and-shoe store Zappos.com. Amazon also owns Audible.com (audio entertainment), Pets.com, and IMDb.com (Internet Movie Database), among others.

## It's not just shopping!

Online banking is also taking off. In 2009, the percentage of adult users in Europe's top five online banking nations were:

| | |
|---|---|
| **87%** | Estonia |
| **87%** | Finland |
| **82%** | Netherlands |
| **79%** | Sweden |
| **77%** | Denmark |

## ONLINE OR IN-STORE?

According to an American survey, in 2009–2010 the percentages of goods people bought online rather than in-store were:

- **74%** electronics
- **74%** music and videos
- **66%** clothing
- **61%** books and magazines
- **48%** computer hardware and software

## 370 million

The number of Taobao users in 2010, when it was one of the top 15 most-visited websites on the planet.

## Did you know?

In 1994, PizzaNet (owned by Pizza Hut) became the first company to offer food delivery over the Internet. The first order is thought to have been for a pepperoni and mushroom pizza with extra cheese.

Internet movie retailer **Netflix** ships out **one million DVDs** to customers every day.

Online shopping is huge in Japan. In 2010, **$185 billion** was spent by Japanese consumers.

**21%** of people in Britain over age 60 claim to do their weekly food shopping online.

British shoppers spent **$8.5 billion** online in November 2009.

Approximately **$115.6 billion** was spent on online travel in the United States in 2009.

## 400 billion yuan

The value of transactions, equal to $61 billion, on Taobao in 2010.

# iTunes

## IN NUMBERS

**10 billion**
In February 2010, iTunes passed a music milestone when the total number of songs sold by the company reached 10 billion.

**2 million**
The number of Beatles songs sold on iTunes in their first week of release in November 2010.

**71**
The age of the person who downloaded iTunes' 10 billionth track, *Guess Things Happen That Way*, by Johnny Cash. The man received a phone call from Apple's Steve Jobs and an iTunes gift card worth $10,000.

**7 billion**
The number of apps (applications) downloaded from the iTunes store as of October 2010.

## 48,000

The number of items sold every minute in 2010 on China's leading e-commerce website, Taobao.

## WHAT DO YOU THINK?

Online consumers rely heavily on reviews. Here are the percentages of global consumers who would not buy certain products without first consulting reviews:

- consumer electronics **40%**
- a car **38%**
- software **28%**
- services **22%**
- cosmetics **21%**

淘宝网
Taobao.com

# A world without wires

More than 100 years ago, radio waves were identified as a method of transmitting signals over long distances without wires. Wi-Fi, short for Wireless Fidelity, is the name for technology that allows digital data to be transmitted using radio signals. Since the 1990s, the world has gone increasingly wireless to deliver mobile Internet connectivity to a massive range of machines, from tablet PCs to washing machines.

## Hotspots

A hotspot is an area of Wi-Fi coverage found in a public area such as a library, city center, or even the International Space Station (below). Most are secured, requiring password access or payment to use the facility. Some are unsecured or deliberately free. You can also use small, portable routers called MiFi to generate personal wireless hotspots that send signals over your mobile phone carrier's network.

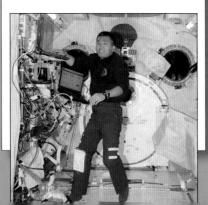

## WiMAX antennae

WiMAX is Wi-Fi that uses powerful radio transmissions to enable signals carrying data to travel distances up to 30 miles (50 km) for fixed WiMAX stations, and 3–9 miles (5–15 km) for mobile stations. It gives moving vehicles broadband levels of Internet access.

## Simple setup

A simple home Wi-Fi setup delivers a broadband Internet connection using a device called a wireless router. This receives data from the Internet and transmits it as a radio signal, usually up to a distance of 100–130 ft (30–40 m) indoors, and a little farther outside.

## Appliance science

Household products, from digital photo frames to refrigerators, are provided with Wi-Fi access as new applications are developed. A Wi-Fi-enabled refrigerator launched in 2011 can stream music into a kitchen, search for recipes online, and even order food from grocery stores.

## Your Wi-Fi world
It's never been easier to get online. Laptops, netbooks, PDAs (palmtop computers), and tablet PCs fitted with a Wi-Fi adaptor can all send and receive signals via wireless routers. Videos and sound can also be streamed to a TV or music system via a wireless home network.

## On course
In 2008, the Yokohama Country Club golf course in Japan installed 50 Inforemer HDX displays in their golf carts. This device features GPS (Global Positioning System) to help golfers measure their shots and navigate the course, and also Wi-Fi, to create a course-wide hotspot.

## Media poles
More than 20 LED (light-emitting diode) displays, 40 ft (12 m) in height, line the streets of the Gangam district of Seoul, South Korea. These "media poles" generate a streetwide Wi-Fi hotspot and offer touch screens so that pedestrians can search maps and read news.

## Did you know?
In 2010, free Wi-Fi hotspots were installed in 820 taxis in Tokyo, Japan. One hundred of these vehicles also include free Sony PSPs for passengers to use during their ride.

## Wi-Fi wear
People who need to connect to the Internet when out and about often use a small device called a scanner that detects local Wi-Fi hotspots without the need to boot up a computer. The scanner can even be built into T-shirts—the logo lights up when a hotspot is found!

## Citywide coverage
Muni-Fi is a large, integrated system of public hotspots that covers much or all of city. In 2005, Sunnyvale, California, became the first city in the United States to offer free citywide Wi-Fi. Other city hotspots include Kuala Lumpur, Malaysia, parts of Paris, France, and Oulu, Finland.

## On the move
Wi-Fi allows people to work and play on the move using their phones and other personal devices. Some cameras or camera phones also use Wi-Fi to "geotag" photos (adding geographical information, such as the location), and upload them directly to a photo-sharing website.

## Did you know?
Hermosa Beach, California, is home to a giant Wi-Fi hotspot that covers the entire length of the beach, as well as 10,000 nearby homes and the 19,000 people who live there.

# Smartphone

Mobile phones have become so sophisticated some are essentially pocket-sized computers. These "smartphones" feature a full-fledged operating system such as iOS, Android, or Symbian, can run thousands of different small programs known as apps, and boast more processing power than many 10-year-old PCs.

## iPhone

Apple's fourth-generation smartphone was launched in 2010. Containing 16 or 32 GB of storage, the phone's steel-and-glass casing measures 4.5 x 2.30 in (11.52 x 5.86 cm) and is just 0.37 in (0.93 cm) thick. Central to smartphones' success is the vast range of apps available. According to Apple, more than 300,000 different apps, from games to business software, now exist for iPhones.

Jack for inserting headphones

Home button assembly

Lower antenna and speaker

30-pin socket connector

Power button and sensor cable

Motor to allow vibration

Plastic frame to protect glass

### 1 Microphone

The iPhone has twin microphones; the main one at the bottom of the phone is used for calls and voice-controlled apps, and a second microphone at the top helps cancel out background noise and make music and calls clearer.

### 2 Screen

The 3.5-in (8.9-cm) liquid crystal display (LCD) is one of the highest-resolution screens around. This allows the device to display ultra-sharp text and graphics. The screen is protected by a layer of glass chemically treated to be 20 times stiffer and 30 times harder than plastic.

### 3 A4 chip

The iPhone's main processor is a complete system on a chip. It has a lot of work to do—from handling the phone's graphics and running multiple apps at the same time, to interpreting touch gestures on its screen and displaying video in real time.

### 4 Camera

There are two cameras featured on the iPhone 4. The rear camera has a 5-megapixel resolution and can be used for capturing both still images and video. The camera on the front of the phone is for use with Apple's video-calling app, FaceTime.

### 5 Lithium-ion battery

A 1420mAh power pack inside the iPhone is rechargeable and gives up to 6 hours of call time, 10 hours of WiFi use to send messages or surf the Internet, and up to 40 hours of audio playback to listen to music, podcasts, or audiobooks.

Steel outer frame acts as antenna

512 megabytes of memory

Micro-SIM card holder

WiFi antenna

Vibration button

Volume up and down buttons

Front-facing VGA camera

plastic frame to house components

Back sheet of ultra-durable glass

# How a touch screen works

### Selection
The latest smartphone screens are touch sensitive. The user swipes a finger across the screen to find the app they want to use, which they open by touching the appropriate icon.

### Touch registered
A grid of sensors below the screen registers the touch as electrical signals. They detect where the touch occurred, and the data is sent as electrical impulses to the processor.

### Gesture recognized
The processor interprets the touch gesture made, matching it to those held in its memory and also checking what that gesture means in any specific app being run at the time.

### Action completed
The gesture has been recognized and the action of launching the app is performed by the phone's processor. This all happens smoothly and in an instant.

# Text talk

Everyone may be talking about the latest technology—multi-touch, multimedia devices, video calls, and photo messaging—but Internet communication is still dominated by messages typed out in text form. Billions of e-mails, text messages, and instant messages are sent every day, and many millions of people update their blogs.

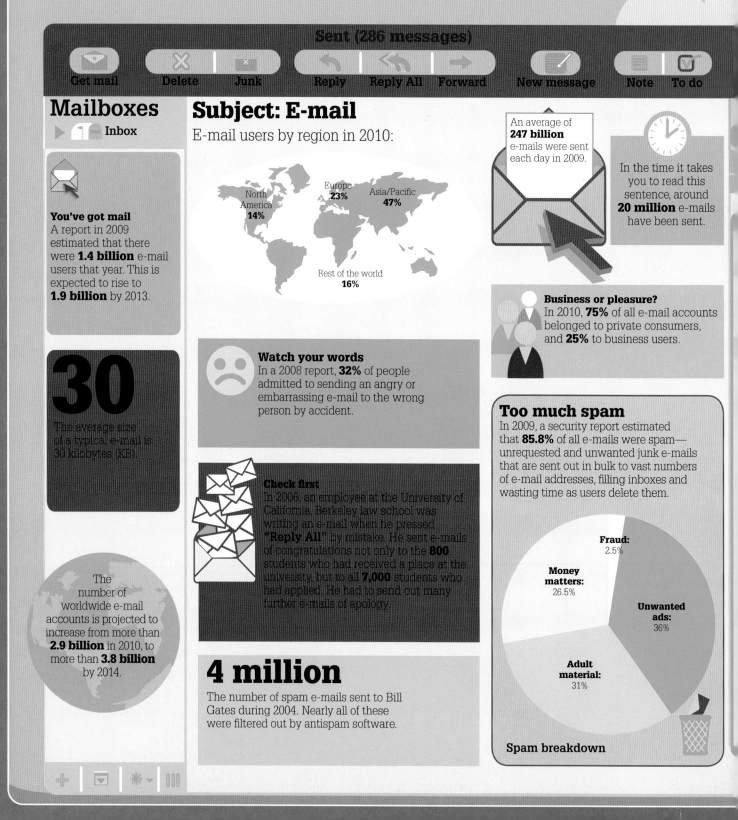

**Sent (286 messages)**

Get mail | Delete | Junk | Reply | Reply All | Forward | New message | Note | To do

## Mailboxes

▶ 🔔 Inbox

**You've got mail**
A report in 2009 estimated that there were **1.4 billion** e-mail users that year. This is expected to rise to **1.9 billion** by 2013.

# 30
The average size of a typical e-mail is 30 kilobytes (KB).

The number of worldwide e-mail accounts is projected to increase from more than **2.9 billion** in 2010, to more than **3.8 billion** by 2014.

## Subject: E-mail

E-mail users by region in 2010:

North America **14%**
Europe **23%**
Asia/Pacific **47%**
Rest of the world **16%**

**Watch your words**
In a 2008 report, **32%** of people admitted to sending an angry or embarrassing e-mail to the wrong person by accident.

**Check first**
In 2006, an employee at the University of California, Berkeley law school was writing an e-mail when he pressed **"Reply All"** by mistake. He sent e-mails of congratulations not only to the **800** students who had received a place at the university, but to all **7,000** students who had applied. He had to send out many further e-mails of apology

# 4 million
The number of spam e-mails sent to Bill Gates during 2004. Nearly all of these were filtered out by antispam software.

An average of **247 billion** e-mails were sent each day in 2009.

In the time it takes you to read this sentence, around **20 million** e-mails have been sent.

**Business or pleasure?**
In 2010, **75%** of all e-mail accounts belonged to private consumers, and **25%** to business users.

**Too much spam**
In 2009, a security report estimated that **85.8%** of all e-mails were spam—unrequested and unwanted junk e-mails that are sent out in bulk to vast numbers of e-mail addresses, filling inboxes and wasting time as users delete them.

Fraud: 2.5%
Money matters: 26.5%
Unwanted ads: 36%
Adult material: 31%

**Spam breakdown**

## Blogs

Starting out as diaries or journals displayed online, blogs get their name from "web log," a term invented by American blogger Jorn Barger in 1997. Blogs consist of posts or entries, which are mostly text but can contain images, videos, or links, with the latest post displayed first.

One in five bloggers update their blogs daily, and more than half operate **two or more blogs**.

Around **60%** of bloggers are between the ages of 18 and 44, and more than **70%** are male.

**49%** The percentage of total bloggers worldwide that are from the United States.

### In numbers

**133 million**
The number of different blogs listed on leading blog directory Technorati since 2002.

**77%** The percentage of Internet users who read blogs.

**15%** An estimated 15% of bloggers spend **10 hours** a week blogging.

**1901** The year the world's oldest blogger, Bernando Lapello, was born. The Brazilian is the author of the **Age Less Live More** blog.

**200 million**
To date, the world's most popular blogger is Chinese writer and rally-car driver Han Han whose blog attracts more than 200 million visitors.

## Text messaging and IM

The short-message service (SMS) featured on mobile phones allows text messages up to 160 characters long to be sent to other mobile users. Texting is big business, with millions signing up for text-alert services to get the latest news or sports scores delivered by text.

The first SMS text ever, sent by engineer Neil Papworth to Vodafone's Richard Jarvis on December 3, 1992, read "Merry Christmas."

There are an estimated **3.6 billion** global users of text messages worldwide.

A staggering **6.1 trillion** text messages were sent in 2010—that's almost 200,000 every second.

According to a study in 2009, **95%** of all text messages are read within 4 to 15 minutes and replied to within the hour.

An average of **11 million** text messages were sent in the United Kingdom every hour during 2009. In the same year, just two countries, the United States and the Philippines, were responsible for 35% of all texts sent.

In 2010, two 23-year-old British climbers trapped 11,500 ft (3,500 m) up western Europe's highest mountain, Mount Blanc, on the border of France and Italy, were rescued after sending a text for help to a friend back in England, who then called the rescue services.

An SMS text message uses **140 bytes** of memory—a typical MP3 song uses the same amount of memory as 4,000 text messages.

Instant messaging (IM) programs are another popular method of communicating between two people using computers. AOL Instant Messenger (AIM) is used by **15.4 million** people each month. On average, users spend 43 minutes on AIM each day.

In 2009, around **40 million** users logged in at the same time during peak hours on Windows Live Messenger, where users can send instant messages to each other.

### TxtMsgs

The 160 character limit for text messages has seen a whole texting language build up, full of unusual abbreviations to save space.

| | |
|---|---|
| **LOL** | laugh out loud |
| **BTW** | by the way |
| **ROFL** | rolling on floor laughing |
| **a2m1** | *A demain*—French for "see you tomorrow" |
| **nph** | *no puedo hablar*—Spanish for "I can't talk now" |
| **GuK** | *Gruß und Kuss*—German for "love and kisses" |

Send

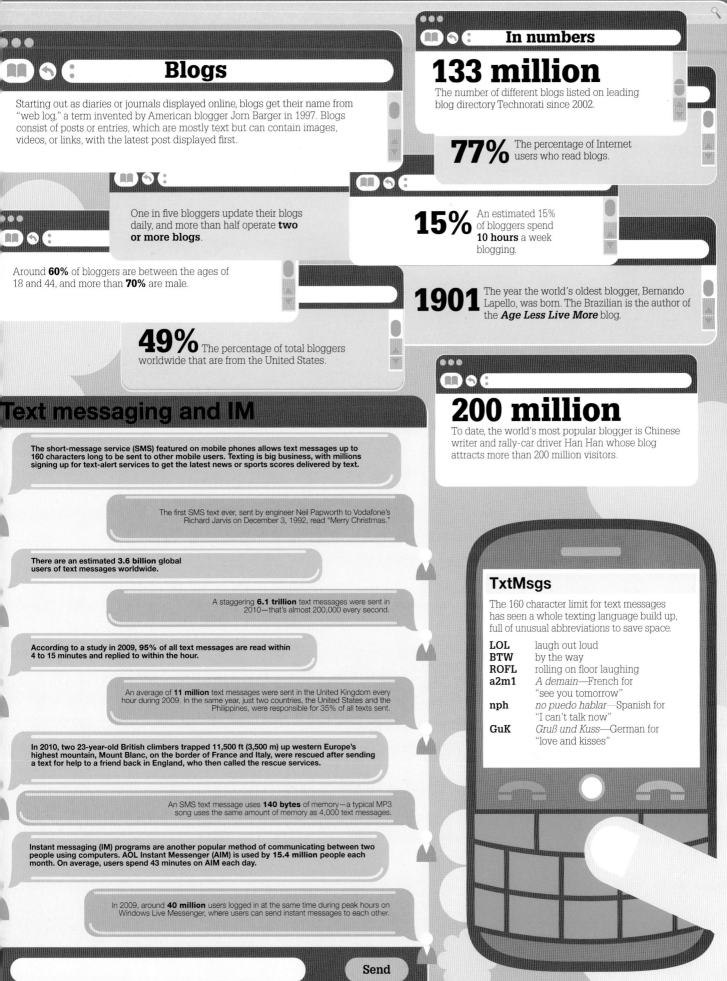

# Eye in the sky

Fifteen years ago, people would have thought you were crazy if you suggested using a PC to fly around a virtual Earth, zooming out to see whole continents, then zooming in to see your own home. Yet, through faster Internet access, better computers, and smart programming, a range of mapping services now allows you to do just that. The Italian city of Rome, for example, can be explored in many different ways.

**Bird's-eye view**
From a distant aerial view of a city or region, many mapping programs allow you to zoom in closer and closer. This clear bird's-eye view gives an interesting perspective on St. Peter's Basilica, inside Vatican City.

**Road maps**
There are a number of detailed street and road map services available for free on the Web. Users can plot routes between different points, zoom in close for individual street directions, and bookmark locations for later use.

**The night sky**
Some mapping programs and web apps turn the focus away from Earth. They observe stars, planets, comets, and other phenomena in the night sky and plot how they shift during a year. Many of these astronomy apps are free.

## Gathering data

Collecting all the imagery for a complete, detailed visual map of all parts of the world is a daunting task. A range of different techniques is used to image the Earth in both close-up and long-distance views.

### On the ground
Google's fleet of street cars, tricycles, and snowmobiles generate ground-level imagery for use with Google Street View. Fitted 8 ft (2.5 m) above the ground on each vehicle's mast are nine cameras that together generate 360-degree views.

### Sharing resources
In some apps, users upload and share their own photos, tagged to locations. This image of Rome's Pantheon is from Panoramio. Within two years of its launch, Panoramio boasted more than five million user-submitted images.

### In the air
Many mapping and virtual world projects use aerial photography taken from low-level aircraft. Photography for bird's-eye-view maps is usually taken from a 45-degree angle to the ground. This helps give a simple, 3-D–like perspective.

### The view on the street
Rome's Trevi Fountain can be seen from ground level using street layers in Bing Maps and Google Earth. These display panoramic photos along various streets in the world but are controversial because of privacy issues.

### Up in space
Landsat satellites have been orbiting our planet since 1972, beaming back thousands of visible-light and infrared images of Earth's surface. These have been used by scientists, environmentalists, and governments, as well as by recent online mapping services.

### Weather view
Satellite weather images were among the first large-scale maps available on the Internet. Data from weather satellites is now incorporated into some mapping programs, so they display clouds over the world in real time.

### Reconstructions in 3-D
Using freely available software, Web users can build and display 3-D models of buildings, such as this reconstruction of the Colosseum. Google has even modeled different tree species and "planted" them across Google Earth.

**Opera House, Sydney, Australia →**
This 3-D image shows the unusual concrete shells that form the distinctive roofs of the Opera House in Sydney Harbour.

**← Manhattan, New York**
This bird's-eye view shows the famous grid system of Manhattan, one of five boroughs in New York City. It is the most populated of all the boroughs.

**Tsunami destruction, Indonesia →**
You can also see changing landscapes. These images show an area of Indonesia before (right) and after (far right) the tsunamis of 2004.

**← Wilkins Ice Shelf, Antarctica**
This 93-mile (150 km) long ice shelf is breaking up and floating away from the Antarctic mainland. An overhead view shows the large chunks of ice that have already broken off.

Lake Titicaca, Peru

**← Mount St. Helens, Washington**
Hover above the large crater of Mount St. Helens, an active volcano that still spouts ash and steam. In 1980, it erupted violently, killing 57 people.

**← Mount Fuji, Japan**
Soar over the snow-covered cone of Japan's highest mountain and one of the country's most famous landmarks. Mount Fuji is a dormant volcano that last erupted in 1708.

**↑ Matterhorn, Italy and Switzerland**
At 14,692 ft (4,478 m), the Matterhorn is one of the highest peaks in the Alps. Shaped like a pyramid, it towers over the border between Italy and Switzerland.

**← Three Gorges Dam, Hubei Province, China**
The largest hydroelectrical dam in the world, the Three Gorges Dam can be seen spanning the Yangtze River. China hopes it will reduce reliance on coal power and help reduce flooding along the river.

**← Hong Kong, China**
Zoom in and look closer at the 3-D skyscrapers of Hong Kong, one of the world's top financial centers. The city's tallest building is the International Commerce Centre at 1,588 ft (484 m).

# Where do you want to go?

**↑ Bird's Nest, Beijing, China**
This spectacular stadium made of steel beams was the center of the 2008 Olympic Games. You can look inside the stadium and see activity inside.

Using software available on the Web, you can explore a virtual Earth that has been put together using images from satellites, aerial photography, and other sources. Travel the planet—below the oceans, over its highest peaks, and even beyond. Earth's natural wonders are all there to see along with world-famous cities and landmarks.

**← Grasberg mine, New Guinea, Indonesia**
Grasberg is the world's largest gold mine and third-largest copper mine. This overhead view, and the buildings around the site, give some idea of its scale.

**Boneyard, Tuscon, Arizona →**
More than 4,000 retired military aircraft can be seen lined up in the Arizona desert. The dry climate prevents the aircraft from deteriorating quickly.

**↑ Wreck of the *Titanic*, Atlantic Ocean**
An undersea, 3-D view allows exploration of shipwrecks. The *Titanic*, an ocean liner that hit an iceberg, sank, and split in two in 1912, is one of the most famous wrecks.

**Mangroves, Bangladesh →**
From high in the sky you can see channels of the River Ganges snake toward the Indian Ocean. This is a huge area of mangrove forest called the Sunderbans.

**← Venice, Italy**
The city of Venice stands on 117 small islands on a marshy lagoon. Instead of roads, there is a system of canals navigated by boats with paths for pedestrians.

**← Uluru, Australia**
This sandstone rock is a sacred site to aboriginal Australians. It looms out of the desert and glows red and orange in the sunlight.

**← Lake Titicaca,
...u and Bolivia**
...h in the Andes ...ntains, at an altitude ...2,500 ft (3,811 m), ...e Titicaca is the ...est lake in South ...erica.

**← Easter Island (Rapa Nui), South Pacific**
Explore Easter Island and find the enormous *mo'ai*, statues built by the Rapa Nui people between the 10th and 17th centuries CE, that stare out to sea.

**→ Hippos, Tanzania**
Some views reveal wildlife in the landscape. Images from a low-flying plane show a large herd of hippos swimming in a river in Tanzania.

**...al Sea, Kazakhstan and Uzbekistan →**
...he rivers that fed the ...huge Aral Sea were ...verted for irrigation ...1960s. Images show ...v the lake has shrunk ...olume between 1989 ...) and 1999 (far right).

**↑ The Pentagon, Virginia**
The headquarters of the U.S. Department of Defense looks impressive from the air. The five-sided structure is the world's largest office building by floor area.

**← Andromeda**
The nearest galaxy to ours is Andromeda, 2.5 million light-years away. It is a spiral galaxy and contains twice as many stars as the Milky Way.

**← Eiffel Tower, Paris, France**
This 3-D view of the Eiffel Tower in Paris shows how the structure dominates the city's skyline. It's the second-largest building in France and was built in 1889.

**↓ Crab Nebula**
Look deep into our galaxy, the Milky Way, and you will find the Crab Nebula, the remains of a star that exploded in the year 1054.

**← Mariana Trench, Pacific Ocean**
You can even dive below the surface of the sea and explore the deepest point on Earth, the Mariana Trench, at a depth of 36,000 ft (11,000 m).

**...Great Barrier ...ef, Australia**
...e world's largest ...ef system can be ...en from outer space. ...stretches more than ...00 miles (2,600 km) ...d teems with a ...verse range of life.

**← Nile Delta, Egypt**
From the air, you can see the Nile River cutting through the vast empty expanse of the Sahara Desert. Fertile green areas line its banks and mark its delta as it reaches the Mediterranean Sea (top).

**← Bosphorus, Turkey**
The Bosphorus Strait is the border between Europe (far left) and Asia (left). Two bridges span the strait, below the center of the image. The strait flows between the Black Sea (top) and the Sea of Marmara (below).

**↑ Santorini, Greece**
Several volcanic islands make up Santorini in the Aegean Sea. A huge volcanic eruption around 3,500 years ago left a huge, sea-filled depression in the center of the islands.

**Olympus Mons, Mars →**
On Mars lies a giant volcano that rises 15 miles (24 km) above the planet's surface. Olympus Mons is the highest mountain in the Solar System.

**↑ Mars**
Head farther out into the Solar System and explore the rusty-red surface of Mars. Tens of thousands of craters mark its surface, created by rocky asteroids that crashed into the planet.

**...t Plains, ...st United States**
...this huge expanse ...nd has been used ...ng or grazing ...k. Where the land ...ater is brought in ...te the land.

**Moon →**
There are many ways to explore the Moon online. You can zoom into its surface, tour the Apollo spacecraft landing sites, and see 3-D models of some of the craft.

**← Lambert Crater, Moon**
Lambert is one of millions of craters on the Moon, many of which have been named. Craters can be up to many hundreds of miles wide.

# What's a wiki?

A wiki is a part of a website that is open so that many different people can contribute to and edit its content. Users can access and edit the page online using their regular web browser. Wikis can be useful in many ways, such as when a group of people from different countries want to work together to produce a single letter or article about a subject. Wiki pages can be easily and quickly updated and usually feature links to other web pages.

## Wikipedia

The biggest, most famous wiki of all is the online encyclopedia Wikipedia. It is a collection of wikis in different languages, more than 260 in total, with the biggest—in the English language—containing more than 3.5 million articles, all available on the Web for free.

## Wales and Sanger

As the new century began, Americans Larry Sanger and Jimmy Wales were involved in building an online encyclopedia called Nupedia. Sanger learned about wikis from a contributor to WikiWikiWeb and convinced Wales and others to try it out. Wikipedia launched in 2001, with 20,000 articles created by the end of that first year.

## The first wiki

Ward Cunningham, an American software developer, began work on the first wiki in 1994. He created an open, editable set of web pages to help programmers and other computer technicians share ideas more efficiently. He added this to his own company's website in 1995.

## Not for profit

Wikipedia is one of the world's top ten most visited websites. If run for profit, advertising on its pages would generate hundreds of millions of dollars. But its founders have resisted turning it into a business, instead relying on fund-raising and donations from individuals and organizations. Both Google and the charity set up by eBay founder, Pierre Omidyar, recently made million-dollar donations.

## Wikileaks

The most controversial of all wikis is the Wikileaks site launched in 2006. It contains private, secret, and classified documents on military, business, and governments leaked to the site, usually by anonymous sources. Wikileaks is now banned in a number of countries.

## Other wikis

Wikis exist for all sorts of subjects including music lyrics (Lyricwiki), medicine (Ask DrWiki), Wikitravel, and *World of Warcraft* (Wowpedia). One of the largest wikis is Hudong, an enormous Chinese online encyclopedia using the wiki format that contains more than three million articles.

## Quick, quick

Cunningham named his first open, editable website WikiWikiWeb after the free shuttle bus that runs from Honolulu airport, Hawaii. WikiWiki means "quick, quick" in Hawaiian.

## Checking sources

Wikipedia can be a tremendous resource but due to errors and pranks, it is recommended that other sources be used to double-check facts. When French composer Maurice Jarre died in 2009, many newspaper articles included a quote from him. However, the quote had been made up and added to Wikipedia by Irish student Shane Fitzgerald.

*"Imagine a world in which every single person on the planet is given free access to the sum of all human knowledge. That's what we're doing."*
*Jimmy Wales, 2004*

### Edit wars

Sometimes, topics elicit strong opinions. An edit war occurs when rival editors keep changing an article to fit their views. Many edit wars are trivial, but some are serious. The Wikipedia entry on the Iraq War, for instance, went through more than 12,000 different edited versions.

## WikiCriticism

Critics point out that some Wikipedia articles are poorly written or involve nonexperts writing about complex topics, and thus may contain confusing language or mistakes. Sometimes people vandalize articles, present opinions as facts, or simply add lies, such as in 2006 when English soccer player David Beckham was defined as an 18th-century Chinese goalkeeper.

### Error-Ridden

In 2005, the scientific journal *Nature* conducted a study comparing 42 science articles in Wikipedia with the online version of *Encyclopaedia Britannica*. The survey revealed that *Britannica* had 123 errors while Wikipedia had 162, an average of 3.9 per article.

## The millionth entry

In March 2006, an entry on Jordanhill railway station in Scotland became the English edition of Wikipedia's one millionth article. Within three and a half years, an additional two million articles were added on every conceivable topic from aardvarks to zippers as well as the smell of new cars, wife-carrying competitions, and National Towel Day!

## How editing works

Behind Wikipedia is a tiny number of paid employees and an enormous community of many thousands of people who give up their leisure time to write and debate new articles, and repair or update existing ones.

⊙ At the top of every page on Wikipedia is an edit button. Clicking on this calls up the page in editable form, complete with codes for formatting the text and adding tables, links, and images.

⊙ Wikipedia has online help guides and a sandbox, where people can experiment. Material in the sandbox is erased automatically every 12 hours. The history tab also shows earlier versions of an article.

⊙ Any edited page can be previewed and saved. Other editors may debate the new article or propose changes on the article's separate talk page.

# The age of the Internet

The Internet developed slowly and organically, as computer and telecom experts pieced together the necessary new technology and software to enable computers of different types to "talk" to each other and form networks. Today, the pace of change on the Internet is incredibly fast. A strong, well-planned website or Internet application can become a global success in just a few months—or even weeks.

**1978**
Gary Thuerk sends the first spam e-mail, advertising DEC computer systems. More than 900 users receive the e-mail and are not amused.

**↓ 1992**
The world's first smartphone, IBM's Simon, is demonstrated and goes on sale to the public the following year. It boasts a touchscreen, calendar, and e-mail features.

**1969**
ARPA's computer network, ARPANET, begins with four locations, called nodes: at the University of Utah, two California universities, and the Stanford Research Institute. A five-letter message was successfully sent an hour later.

**↓ 1988**
American student Robert Tappan Morris creates the Morris worm, one of the first major computer security attacks, which disrupts parts of the Internet. Morris receives a three-year suspended sentence and a fine of $10,000,

**↓ 1974**
In *A Protocol for Packet Network Interconnection*, Vinton Cerf and Bob Kahn explain the software (now developed as TCP/IP) that would allow different computers and networks to communicate with each other to form an "inter-network."

**↓ 1982**
The smiley emoticon :-) is proposed by U.S. computer scientist Scott Fahlman on Carnegie Mellon University's bulletin boards.

**↓ 1957**
The Soviet Union launches the first satellite, *Sputnik*. In response, the U.S. sets up the Advanced Research Projects Agency (ARPA) to fund research into technology.

**1988**
In Finland, Jarkko Oikarinen launches the multi-user chat program IRC (Internet Relay Chat), a forerunner of online instant messaging.

**1990**
The first search engine, called Archie, is created by Alan Emtage, a student at McGill University in Montreal, Canada.

**1967**
The UK's National Physical Laboratory develops packet switching—a way of sending data over a network by breaking it up into small units, or packets.

**↑ 1971**
American computer programmer Ray Tomlinson starts the first e-mail system on ARPANET. He uses the @ symbol to identify unique users and sends the first e-mail message.

**1977**
U.S. businessmen Dennis Hayes and Dale Heatherington develop the personal computer modem (a device that connects you to the Internet) and sell it to computer hobbyists.

**1979**
The online discussion board Usenet launches. It allows people to send posts to different newsgroups, divided into topics.

**1984**
The domain name system is introduced, making addresses on the Internet more informative and easier to remember.

**↓ 1989**
Tim Berners-Lee begins work on the World Wide Web while working at CERN, Switzerland.

**1991**
In England, the first webcam is set up in Cambridge University's computer lab. It films a coffee machine so that researchers can see if the pot is empty or not without leaving their seats. The webcam stays switched on until 2001.

**1993**
The Mosaic web browser is released. It is credited with popularizing early use of the World Wide Web.

In February 2005, three former PayPal employees—Chad Hurley, Steve Chen, and Jawed Karim—started to build a video website. The very first clip uploaded in April (and still on the site) shows Karim at the San Diego Zoo. YouTube launched in November 2005. By July 2006, 65,000 new videos were being added every day. Less than a year after its launch, YouTube was sold to Google.

# "I'd like to know what the Internet is going to look like in 2050. Thinking about it makes me wish I were eight years old."

**Vinton Cerf,** 2008, American computer scientist and Internet pioneer

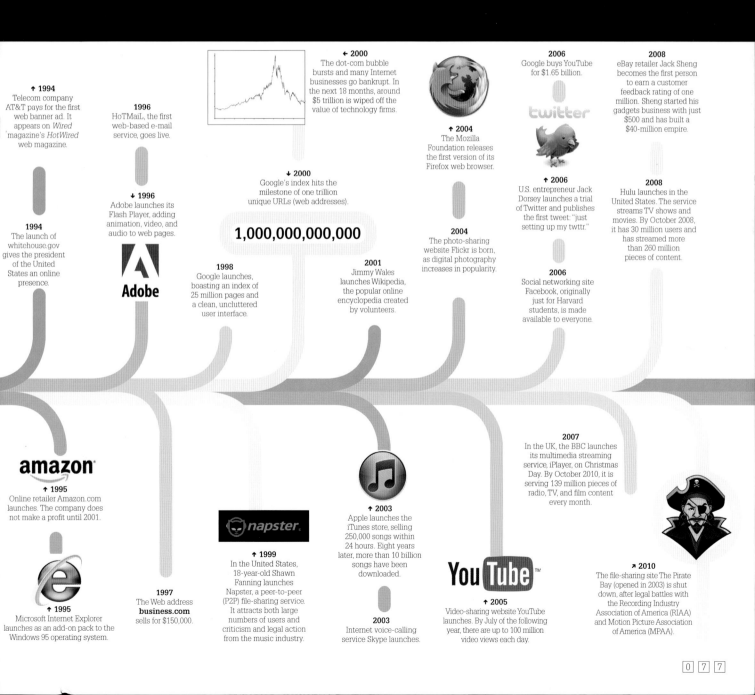

**↑ 1994**
Telecom company AT&T pays for the first web banner ad. It appears on *Wired* magazine's *HotWired* web magazine.

**1996**
HoTMaiL, the first web-based e-mail service, goes live.

**← 2000**
The dot-com bubble bursts and many Internet businesses go bankrupt. In the next 18 months, around $5 trillion is wiped off the value of technology firms.

**2006**
Google buys YouTube for $1.65 billion.

**2008**
eBay retailer Jack Sheng becomes the first person to earn a customer feedback rating of one million. Sheng started his gadgets business with just $500 and has built a $40-million empire.

**↑ 2004**
The Mozilla Foundation releases the first version of its Firefox web browser.

**1994**
The launch of whitehouse.gov gives the president of the United States an online presence.

**↓ 1996**
Adobe launches its Flash Player, adding animation, video, and audio to web pages.

**↓ 2000**
Google's index hits the milestone of one trillion unique URLs (web addresses).

**1,000,000,000,000**

**↑ 2006**
U.S. entrepreneur Jack Dorsey launches a trial of Twitter and publishes the first tweet: "just setting up my twttr."

**2008**
Hulu launches in the United States. The service streams TV shows and movies. By October 2008, it has 30 million users and has streamed more than 260 million pieces of content.

**1998**
Google launches, boasting an index of 25 million pages and a clean, uncluttered user interface.

**2001**
Jimmy Wales launches Wikipedia, the popular online encyclopedia created by volunteers.

**2004**
The photo-sharing website Flickr is born, as digital photography increases in popularity.

**2006**
Social networking site Facebook, originally just for Harvard students, is made available to everyone.

**↑ 1995**
Online retailer Amazon.com launches. The company does not make a profit until 2001.

**2007**
In the UK, the BBC launches its multimedia streaming service, iPlayer, on Christmas Day. By October 2010, it is serving 139 million pieces of radio, TV, and film content every month.

**↑ 2003**
Apple launches the iTunes store, selling 250,000 songs within 24 hours. Eight years later, more than 10 billion songs have been downloaded.

**↑ 1999**
In the United States, 18-year-old Shawn Fanning launches Napster, a peer-to-peer (P2P) file-sharing service. It attracts both large numbers of users and criticism and legal action from the music industry.

**↗ 2010**
The file-sharing site The Pirate Bay (opened in 2003) is shut down, after legal battles with the Recording Industry Association of America (RIAA) and Motion Picture Association of America (MPAA).

**↑ 1995**
Microsoft Internet Explorer launches as an add-on pack to the Windows 95 operating system.

**1997**
The Web address **business.com** sells for $150,000.

**↑ 2005**
Video-sharing website YouTube launches. By July of the following year, there are up to 100 million video views each day.

**2003**
Internet voice-calling service Skype launches.

**→ Robot helper**
Preserving past media for the future in digital form is a massive job. The Qidenus robotic digitizer turns and scans book pages with perfect accuracy. It can scan an amazing 2,500 pages per hour with no human intervention.

## Digitizing hard copy

Not long ago, hard copy was king. Everything was written down, typed, printed, photocopied, or filed on paper. Then came the rise of computing and the Internet. These days, most new documents and many books are created in electronic form. At the same time, older materials are being scanned to create digital versions that can be kept on computers. Digital files can be stored by the millions and sent over the Internet in seconds.

**→ In the library**
Libraries of the past held vast quantities of books, newspapers, and journals. Today, many libraries are restricting their physical collections in order to give space to PCs or terminals that offer Internet access.

**← E-readers**
Weighing less than one printed book, an e-reader can hold up to 5,000 books in electronic form. It offers on-the-go portability as well as time-saving features, such as fast keyword searches through millions of words.

# The shift to digital media

Magazines, photos, books, and CDs are all physical media—unlike digital files, they take up a lot of space, take time to be delivered after ordering, are difficult to update, and can be bulky to carry. For these reasons, there has been a huge shift from physical to digital media that can be stored on electronic systems.

**→ MP3 player**
Portable digital music players are memory chips or mini hard drives linked to a small sound card and an amplifier. This 16 GB iPod nano, launched in 2010, holds 4,000 tracks and weighs a mere 0.75 oz (21 g).

## Music media

After decades of vinyl records, compact discs (CDs) arrived in the 1980s. The big shift to digital media, however, came with the ability to copy individual CD tracks into digital formats, such as MP3, WAV, or FLAC files. At last, music was easy to store, play, and share over the Internet. Today, billions of tracks are downloaded from pay sites, such as iTunes and Amazon.

**← Record store**
A large record store held thousands of LPs—dinner-plate-sized vinyl disks that featured 20 to 40 minutes of music per side. Today, music stores mostly sell CDs, but tracks are increasingly bought online instead.

## What's on the tube?

TV has come a long way since the first fuzzy screens appeared in a few wealthy people's homes in the 1930s. TiVo, launched in 1999, was one of the first digital video recorders (DVRs) with a hard drive. Linked to the Internet, the latest DVRs can call up television schedules and pause or rewind live shows. Increasingly, however, many people are not watching television sets at all, viewing programs and movies over the Internet instead.

**→ TV times**
Up until the mid-1950s, television sets showed programs only in black-and-white. They offered just one or two channels, which broadcast programs for just a few hours a day.

**← Streamed content**
iPads and similar digital devices can display streamed video content. They use Wi-Fi or a mobile Internet connection to access websites that offer video clips, full TV shows, or feature-length movies.

**← YouTube**
Many people catch up with TV highlights on video-sharing websites. YouTube is now so influential that President Barack Obama has made exclusive appearances on it.

# E-reader

E-books are books in a digital format, such as a word-processing document or a PDF (portable document file), that can be read on a computer, tablet, or smartphone. E-readers are devices devoted to storing and displaying e-books and other text documents. They allow students, travelers, and commuters to carry large numbers of books, newspapers, PDFs, and other documents in one small package.

E-ink pearl display

37-key round-button keyboard

Four-direction cursor controller

E-ink controller chip

1

2

## Amazon Kindle

Amazon's third-generation Kindle was launched in 2010. At 9 oz (247 g), it weighs less than most paperbacks, yet its 4 GB of memory can hold an astonishing 3,500 books. The device can synchronize with Amazon's Kindle store, allowing users to browse the opening chapters of hundreds of thousands of books, buy books electronically, and download them straight onto the device.

7.5 in x 4.8 in
(190 mm x 123 mm)

0.3 in
(8.5 mm)

## 1 Keyboard

Users can type in a word to look up its meaning in the Kindle's built-in dictionary. Annotations can also be typed into a book, which are stored in the memory. The Alt key allows certain shortcuts and also launches a surprise *Minesweeper* game to play.

## 2 Speakers

The Kindle's two small speakers can output MP3 sound files, such as music or audiobooks. In addition, an experimental feature on the device can convert the text of a book into speech to read a book aloud.

## 3 Battery

A 1750mAh lithium-polymer battery takes up much of the space inside the Kindle case. Due to the very low power demands of the e-ink screen, and with no hard disk to keep spinning, the battery can last up to four weeks between charges.

## 4 Micro-USB port

Books and documents can be moved to the Kindle from a computer via the micro-USB port, which doubles as the way in which the Kindle's battery is charged in around 4.5 hours.

## 5 Logic board

The Kindle's logic board (printed circuit board) contains 4 GB of memory, an e-ink controller chip built by Epson, and a multimedia processor. There is also a chip devoted to managing the unit's power and a Wolfson stereo codec chip to help power the Kindle's twin speakers.

## 6 Wi-Fi card

An Atheros AR6102G 802.11bg chip allows books, newspapers, and other documents to be delivered wirelessly to the Kindle using Amazon's Whispernet data service. A typical book takes under a minute to load onto the machine.

Graphite outer casing

*"The vision is that you should be able to get any book—not just any book in print, but any book that's ever been in print—on this device."*
*Jeff Bezos (2007)*

Jeff Bezos founded Amazon in 1994 to sell books over the Internet. It has grown to become America's largest online retailer and, in 2007, released its first Kindle e-reader.

## E-ink

Unlike laptop and smartphone screens, an e-ink display doesn't fade or wash out in bright sunlight and is easy on the eyes when reading. The display is a plastic film coated with millions of tiny microcapsules. Each capsule contains positively charged white particles and negatively charged black particles. When a grid of electrodes below the film activates, signals in the grid attract one type of particle and repel the other. The repelled particles move to the top of the capsule, where they are visible to the human eye.

White particles attracted to grid
Black particles repelled to top
Grid electrodes have negative charge

White particles repelled to top
Black particles attracted to grid
E-ink capsule full of clear fluid
Grid electrodes have positive charge

# Augmented reality

Using a smartphone, digital tablet, or similar device, an interactive environment of sound, music, photos, video, and text can blend with your surroundings to create a real-time, information-rich connection between you and the world. This is augmented reality (AR), an exciting area of development that may revolutionize how we relate to both technology and the world around us.

## ⬈ How it works

There are different ways to create AR. Usually, an application scans an image or scene, then calls up additional information using a data connection.

⊙ Many AR applications designed for use on the go exploit a mobile device's GPS (Global Positioning System) technology, internal compass or tracking sensors, and camera. Together, these can figure out where the device is, the direction it is facing, and what it is looking at.

⊙ Linking to the Internet through dedicated databases or web searches, the AR application pulls up relevant information and other media, such as videos, to display as layers on-screen.

## ⬈ AR applications

⊙ Columbia University's ARMAR system is testing AR in engineering. As a technician looks at a machine, labels of its parts and videos of repair and fitting techniques appear on the head-mounted display.

⊙ In the future, social networking may get an AR makeover. Pointing your device at people could match them up with photos on the Internet to call up their Facebook page and Twitter account.

⊙ AR books are already with us. When pointed at a webcam, they can link to the Internet to generate 3-D on-screen animations, such as a dinosaur roaming the page.

**Landmarks**
Local attractions are mapped and detailed. Unlike in a printed guidebook, the information can be truly up to the minute, giving the opening hours for that day, plus details of special exhibitions or events and their availability.

Keizersgracht
0.4 miles (0.6 km)

**Food and drink**
Clicking on a food, drink, or accommodation icon calls up nearby restaurants, cafés, bars, hotels, and hostels. Automatic Internet links provide reviews, tips, and in some cases daily specials, discounts, and prices.

Landmarks   Restaurants   Banks

# AR in Amsterdam

A tablet PC displays the AR app Layar and its view of part of the Dutch city of Amsterdam. Layar offers a range of functions, from identifying tweets from people nearby to pointing at a building to see if any companies inside are offering jobs. The data is displayed as layers on-screen that can be turned on and off.

# Just the beginning

Could this be the end of the handset? SixthSense can project a working phone or calculator number pad onto your hand. It is still in development, but in the future, wearable projecting AR devices may be used in education, the military, business, or just for fun.

### Transportation
To answer any transportation questions, the app displays the nearest bus and train stops and lists times. In cities with bicycles for rent, you can locate the nearest rental facility and find out how many bikes are available.

### Utilities
Useful applications can direct you back to your car, and help you find the nearest open drug store, free Wi-Fi, or locksmith. You can even point your camera at a public building to call up photos of the interior.

**Car finder**
2.1 miles (3.4 km)
(17 mins remaining)

Head north for
0.6 miles (1 km) until
you reach a bridge.
Head east for
1.5 miles (2.4 km) until
you reach your car.

### Visitor attractions
Themed tourist-walk layers can give you interactive directions as you move around the city. Providing an audio and video guide, they can focus on a particular attraction, giving photos, Web links, and other details.

★★★★★

**Centraal Station**
1.2 miles (2.0 km)

Gaasperplas

Geln

Westwijk

| Car location | Transportation | Wi-Fi | Shops | Restrooms | Hotels |

# From arcades to
# consoles

Almost no one played video games in the 1960s. The first computer action game, 1961's *Space War!*, required access to a PDP-1 mainframe, which cost more than $120,000 and was found only in a handful of large organizations. Fortunately, one of those organizations was the University of Utah, where a young Nolan Bushnell was studying. He racked up plenty of playing hours and went on to pioneer the introduction of computer games into arcades and, later, people's homes.

## Did you know?

As a science-mad teenager, Bushnell built a liquid-fuel rocket mounted on a roller skate. Unfortunately, it exploded and nearly burned down the family garage!

## Nolan Bushnell

After studying electrical engineering at the University of Utah, Nolan Bushnell (born 1943) began working at Ampex, the electronics company that invented video tape. There, he met engineer Ted Dabney, with whom he formed Syzygy in 1971. The company changed its name to Atari the following year.

## Arcade action

In 1970, Bushnell and Dabney began to develop an arcade game version of *Space War!* The result, *Computer Space*, was brought out by Nutting Associates in 1971. It was the first mass-produced arcade computer game, with around 1,500 machines built.

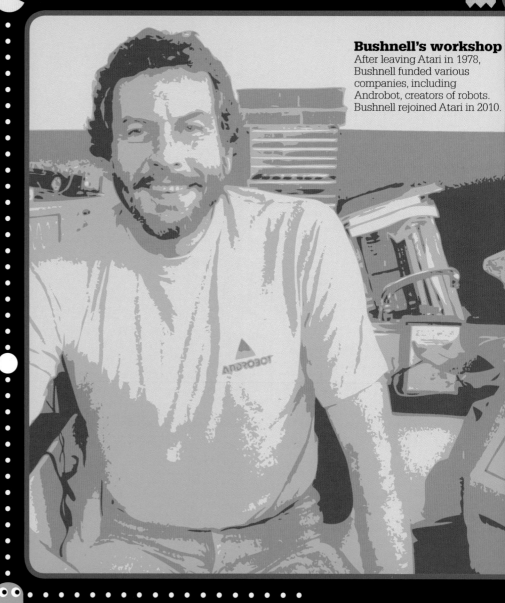

## Bushnell's workshop

After leaving Atari in 1978, Bushnell funded various companies, including Androbot, creators of robots. Bushnell rejoined Atari in 2010.

## Pong

In September 1972, Atari produced its first arcade game, *Pong*. Bushnell and Dabney built the game using a store-bought television, a coin mechanism from a laundromat, and a milk carton used to catch the coins. The debut machine was so popular that it overflowed with quarters and broke down. More than 30,000 *Pong* arcade machines would be sold.

> "The simple, classic games, where we didn't have those graphics to fall back on, had to be really well-tuned, and the response times had to be honed. We focused more on game play than I think people do today."
>
> *Nolan Bushnell, 2009*

## Top-selling Atari 2600 games

1 *Pac-Man*
2 *Pitfall!*
3 *Missile Command*
4 *Demon Attack*
5 *E.T. the Extra-Terrestrial*
6 *Atlantis*
7 *Adventure*
8 *River Raid*
9 *Kaboom!*
10 *Space Invaders*

## A console classic

In 1977, the Atari 2600 video console was launched with just 128 bytes of built-in memory (a CD contains more than 700 million). The machine came with two paddles (above), two joysticks, and a simple *Combat* shooting game. Additional games were sold on cartridges containing just 4 K (later 16 K) of memory. After a slow start, sales boomed. In 1980, Atari racked up $2 billion in sales, including millions of consoles and games such as *Pac-Man*, *Space Invaders*, and *Pitfall!*—one of the first successful platform games.

## Atari innovation

Atari was more than a one-trick pony. Its 400, 800, and XT home computers sold well, and the 1989 Atari Lynx (right) was the first handheld game console with a backlit color LCD screen. Able to link with and play against other machines, the Lynx was well ahead of its time but sold poorly compared to its main rival, the Game Boy.

## Did you know?

The three founders of Apple—Steve Jobs, Steve Wozniak, and Ronald Wayne—all previously worked for Atari. Steve Wozniak developed the prototype of the smash-hit Atari game, *Breakout*.

# Early games

On its release in 1981, the shoot-'em-up game *Galaga* (below) with its blocky color graphics, swooping streams of aliens, and chorus of bleeps coming from its one speaker was considered state of the art. Gaming has changed enormously since early arcade and home games, yet those old games still retain their addictive appeal. On New Year's Day 2011, Andrew Laidlaw set a *Galaga* world-record tournament score of 4,525,150 points.

## Game worlds

The game of *Galaga* was just a single screen across which different waves of aliens descended. Like many early games, it had just three controls: left, right, and fire. Since then, both game play and game worlds have mushroomed in scale, size, and complexity. *Anarchy Online*, for example, has a 112-page manual of instructions for its "getting started" section alone, while *Tiger Woods PGA Tour 11* includes accurate 3-D models of 27 complete real-life golf courses.

## Arcade play

In the beginning, the only place most people were able to play video games was in a noisy arcade among crowds of other players. You often had to line up for the most popular games, and needed a pocketful of quarters.

## Sounds good

Early games were silent or merely bleeped. Then, in 1980, an arcade game called *Rally X* became one of the first to feature background music. Later the same year, the game *Stratovox* surprised players with voice-synthesized speech. Modern games have complex soundtracks and tens of thousands of lines of speech, far more than a typical movie.

## HIGH SCORE
00

## 1OP
00

## Great graphics

Processing power has increased sharply, and most modern computers and consoles feature high-speed graphics cards. Incredibly realistic 3-D worlds, scenes, and characters are now standard in many games.

GAME OVER

CREDIT 0

"When Taito saw the prototype [of *Space Invaders*], they said, 'You can't shoot people! And you must not create the image of war.' So I changed the characters into monsters. At the time, I was trying to decide what the focus would be, and had heard of a sci-fi movie being produced in America called *Star Wars.* I thought a space fad might be on the way and decided to focus on aliens. And that's how the monsters became the invaders that are known today."

*Tomohiro Nishikado*

*Joining Japanese pinball and vending-machine company Taito in 1969, Tomohiro Nishikado (born 1944) designed a number of Japan's early arcade games before releasing* Space Invaders *in 1978. One of the first addictive, action-shooter games, it caused a sensation and inspired other designers. Taito sold* Space Invader *consoles in Japan and the United States and then, in 1980, brought the game into millions of homes by transfering it to the Atari 2600 console. It is still played today.*

# The story of
# Nintendo

→ **Donkey Kong**
Where it all began in 1981! Created for arcade machines, *Donkey Kong* launched Miyamoto's career and kick-started Nintendo's dominance.

Once upon a time, Nintendo was just a humble maker of playing cards in Kyoto, Japan. One hundred and twenty years later, it's one of its country's biggest success stories. It's a giant in the video game industry, with products found in homes the world over. It's safe to say that Nintendo has played an important role in shaping the way that we interact with computer games today.

← **NES**
In 1983, the company's first cartridge-game system, the Nintendo Entertainment System, sold all over the world. It overtook the Atari 2600 as the market leader.

→ **Super Mario**
Originally named "Jumpman," Mario is arguably the world's most recognizable cartoon character—just as famous as Mickey Mouse.

↓ **Pokémon**
Since first appearing in 1996, games featuring these "pocket monsters" have together sold around 200 million copies.

## Origins

People think of Nintendo as a cutting-edge company, but it was actually founded in 1889 to manufacture cards for Hanafuda, a popular Japanese card game. In the 1960s, Nintendo branched out, running taxis and making instant rice meals. In the 1970s, it sold its first toys and video games. Nintendo produced its first handheld electronic game, the Game & Watch, in 1980.

## Shigeru Miyamoto

As the creator of *Donkey Kong*, Mario, *The Legend of Zelda*, and the Wii, Shigeru Miyamoto (born 1952) may be responsible for more man-hours lost to gaming than anyone in history! Miyamoto, who joined Nintendo as its first staff artist in 1977, is now responsible for every Nintendo game and has been dubbed the "Walt Disney" of the video game industry.

**↑ SNES**
In 1990, the Super Nintendo Entertainment System arrived with double the processing power of the NES, allowing a big leap forward in game quality.

## Studio supervisor

Miyamoto's mentor was Gunpei Yokoi, originally hired by Nintendo in 1965 to repair conveyor belts and other assembly-line parts. Yokoi went on to invent the Game Boy and to supervise the making of both *Donkey Kong* and Mario.

**→ Game Boy**
Released in 1989 with the classic game *Tetris*, the Game Boy blasted away its handheld opposition. With more than 118 million sold, it's one of the best-selling gaming devices of all time.

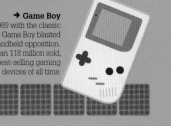

**→ GameCube**
Launched in 2001, the GameCube was Nintendo's first console to use discs instead of cartridges.

## Nintendo by numbers

**4,130**
The number of people who are employed by Nintendo worldwide

**649**
The number of species of Pokémon

**135.6 million**
The number of DS machines sold worldwide from 2004 to October 2010

**1 in 5**
The number of people in Japan who own a model of the Nintendo DS

**$15.2 billion**
Nintendo's total revenue for 2009

**1,068,000**
The highest *Donkey Kong* score so far, achieved by 35-year-old plastic surgeon Hank Chien in 2011

**25**
The number of years since the release of the first *Super Mario* game

**1st**
Miyamoto's rank in *Time* magazine's list of the world's 100 most influential people in 2008

**2.5**
The number of Nintendo consoles sold every second in the United States during Thanksgiving week, 2009

**← N64**
Released in Japan in 1996, the N64 was the first 64-bit console in the world, and raised the standards for 3-D graphics.

**→ The Legend of Zelda**
Introduced in 1997, Link (right) is the main character in *The Legend of Zelda*. He has tried to rescue Princess Zelda in 17 different games.

**← Nintendo DS/DS Lite**
The DS, launched in 2004, was the first gaming device to have a microphone, built-in Wi-Fi, and dual screens, one of which had a touch interface.

**→ Nintendo Wii**
In 2006, Nintendo introduced the Wii, which brought motion control to games and introduced a whole new generation of people to video games.

# The evolution of game controllers

Game controllers allow players to interact with and influence events on screen. Early games were slow-paced—with few moves available to the player, designers gave little thought to the quality or versatility of the controllers. As games have grown more complex, so have the ways to control them. There is now a multi-million-dollar market for the game pads, force-feedback joysticks, and motion-sensing devices that give players the edge in split-second encounters.

↗ **Specialized controllers**

## Did you know?

A special single-player controller was produced for the Japanese robot tanks game *Steel Battalion*. It had two joysticks, three foot pedals, and 40 buttons.

## Type it in

Once upon a time, home computer games used a humble keyboard as their controller. Text adventures called for phrases or sentences to be typed in. Today, there are dedicated gaming keyboards, such as the Razer BlackWidow, which are often backlit for use at night. Their keys are responsive and tough enough to take a pounding. Some can be programmed so that pressing one key has the same effect as pressing several other keys at once.

## Paddles

Atari's groundbreaking early games, such as *Pong* and *Breakout*, were played with paddles—controllers featuring a turning wheel and one or more fire buttons. Each paddle allowed movement along one axis. The trackball was another controller used in early gaming, for example in the shoot-'em-up *Centipede*. Similar to an upside-down mouse, it had a large ball that was rolled by hand to create movement along two axes.

## Joysticks

Early joysticks were four-way movement controllers with a single fire button. Over time, these evolved into more complex and versatile devices. Modern joysticks boast multiple "hot" buttons that can be programmed to perform different game functions. Most joysticks have a hat switch on top of the handle. When activated, this can change the view—allowing the player to look around the game world, for example.

Some games require controllers that break the mold of game pads and joysticks. Here are some of the most popular ones.

## ○ Flight simulators
Mimicking the controls of a light aircraft, flight sims have a hand-operated control column and a foot-controlled rudder bar.

## ○ Voice control
Karaoke games such as *SingStar* rely on a microphone linked to the console to measure a player's singing prowess. Microphones are also used in war games such as *EndWar*, so that players can issue voice commands to their troops.

## ○ Musical instruments
*Guitar Hero* games have a guitar-shaped controller with five colored fret buttons and a strum bar.

## ○ Dance mats
Mats fitted with pressure sensors allow people to play dance games, stepping in sync with the commands on the screen.

## ○ Balance boards
The Wii Fit balance board uses load sensors to detect a player's position and track movements as weight is shifted from one part of the board to another.

## ○ Steering wheels
Many driving games are controlled with a steering wheel. Some feature foot pedals, gear sticks, and indicators as well.

## Did you know?
A limited edition of the third-person shooter *Resident Evil 4* came with a gruesome game pad in the shape of a bloodstained chainsaw.

# Game pads

Game pads feature a series of action and fire buttons around their body, along with a direction controller—usually a four-arrow D-pad (directional pad) or analog stick (a small, sensitive joystick). Game pads arrived once game play demanded many options. Some feature force feedback, in which motors make the game pad move or vibrate in the hand in response to certain actions, such as when the player fires a machine gun.

# Motion sensors

The motion-sensing Wii remote (or Wiimote) contains accelerometers that detect changes in movement along three different axes (up and down, side to side, and forward and back). Accelerometers work whether the controller is held horizontally like a gun or vertically like a golf club. The system determines the exact position of the controller using beams of infrared light projected from the sensor bar next to the screen.

# Your body!

Kinect for the Xbox 360 is the first in a new breed of hands-free controllers. It projects a continuous, coded infrared light beam across the playing space in front of the screen. Then it measures how the light returns in order to build up a 3-D picture of the playing area and any player movements. With a controller like Kinect, players can take part in games just by moving and making gestures. The device also responds to spoken commands.

# Kinect

Nintendo's Wii laid down the motion sensing gauntlet to all comers, but Kinect for the Xbox 360 is a whole different game. The device is a horizontal sensor bar that detects and measures a player's position and movements within a 3-D space in front of the screen. As a result, players can run, jump, throw, and play a new range of controller-free yoga, dance, sports, and action-adventure games.

**Front**

XBOX 360

## You are the controller

There's no game pad, joystick, or motion-sensing wand to grip as you play Kinect. Instead, the device detects and tracks 48 points on each player's body. Gestures such as waving a hand to change screens, as well as movements such as kicking and throwing, are recognized and translated into actions.

5

3

1

2

Front cover with openings for sensors

Casing for electric fan

IR beam maps players body

## How it works

A technique called depth mapping is used to determine an object's location and its distance from Kinect. Sensors and processors send out beams of infrared (IR) light with each small block of light given a code for its location. The light is collected and measured after it has bounced off objects in the scene. From this data, embedded software on processors inside the Kinect create a detailed 3-D depth map.

Circuit board controllers

Accelerometer to determine tilt angle

Plastic casing

**"Kinect just opens up so many opportunities to us because it removes a layer between you and the game."**
*Nick Burton, 2010*

Nick Burton is the Kinect development director at software developers Rare, involved in some of the 17 games released at the time of Kinect's launch.

4

Audio controller chip

Support allows Kinect to swivel

Motor base cover

### 1 RGB camera
This color camera is used for video chat with other Xbox users, and scans your face to see if it matches a face it contains in its memory, allowing facial-recognition login. Some Kinect games also use the camera to take and display onscreen images of you as you play.

### 2 IR Projector and depth sensor
The device's IR laser projector shines beams of infrared light outward. These bounce off surfaces in the room and are collected by the depth sensor, an infrared light camera. Working with the processor, the sensor builds a 3-D depth map, accurate to a depth of 0.4 in (1 cm).

### 3 Microphones
Four downward-facing microphones gather voice commands from the user, recognizing speech in a range of languages and accents. Just saying, "Xbox" calls up a range of commonly used voice commands including "Xbox pause" to pause music or video.

### 4 PrimeSense PS1080-A2
This complete image-processing system on a chip reacts to the data it receives from the depth sensor. It creates a complete depth map of the scene in front of it and can track a number of joints in a player's body at a rate of 30 times per second.

### 5 Motor
Since rooms vary in size and Kinect can be placed above or below a TV screen, the cameras in the sensor bar need to move up or down to adjust its field of view. The motor in the unit's base can tilt the sensors up or down by up to 30 degrees.

**07:00**

**2:00**

## 1 Connecting

Players join a game by subscribing or paying a set fee. They download software onto their computer, known as "the client." Before play can begin, the client must connect to a server.

## 2 Sending

The client computer's signal travels across the world via fiber-optic cable until it reaches the server. Then the server sends a signal back to the client computer, informing the player that a connection has been established.

**Client**

**North America**

**Relay point**

### Did you know?

*EVE Online* is a space game in which players explore a universe of more than 7,500 star systems. On June 6, 2010, more than 60,000 players were all logged on to *EVE* at the same time.

## Limiting lag

Lag is when messages take too lo to reach all the clients. Lengthy la can be lethal in quick-fire comba games. Players limit lag by makin sure their computers run fast and only logging on to speedy server that offer a good connection.

**Relay point**

**South America**

# Playing together

Not so long ago, if you wanted to play a computer game with or against other people, they had to be in the same room. Today, you can play as a wizard or warlord in Washington, Wisconsin, or Warsaw and battle adversaries in Africa, Asia, or Australia. Millions of players around the world are ready to join you or play against you in thousands of online multiplayer games. All you need is a computer or gaming device that is connected to the game's network.

### Did you know?

In the two years after the release of action game *Halo 2*, more than four billion games were played on its servers worldwide, almost 5.5 million games a day.

## 3 Distributing

As the game is played, players' locations and actions are tracked by the game server. When a player moves, fires a weapon, or types a message to another player, an update or "state-of-the-world" message is sent to the server.

## 5 Sending back

The other players' responses travel back to the server and the process begins all over again. All of this takes place in a split second, and it keeps on happening every second of the day.

Europe

Asia

Server

Relay point

Relay point

Africa

## 4 Receiving

The state-of-the-world messages are sent to all players logged into the game. The client computers immediately process the messages and produce graphics, text, and sound to show the latest actions on-screen. Then the other players can respond to what they see.

## On and on...

The game featured here runs on a centralized server that is operational 24 hours a day, allowing players to come and go. As Australian gamers finally head off to bed, American players may just be getting up and logging on.

Australia

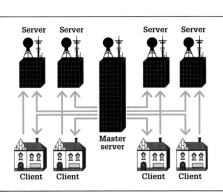

## Distributed servers

Complex games, particularly fast-paced action games such as *Halo* that require frequent status messages, spread the load across multiple smaller servers rather than just one centralized server. When players log on to the game, a master server provides a list of available smaller servers for the client to connect to in order to play.

Server   Server   Server   Server

Master server

Client   Client   Client   Client

# How video games are made

That disc you slide into your game console is the product of huge teams and big budgets. When *Doom* was released in 1993, industry insiders were stunned that a game could cost $200,000 to make. A modern game budget can be 200 times that. To produce the smash shooter *Call of Duty: Black Ops*, game developer Teyarch had 250 employees working for two years.

## ESRB ratings

The United States is the biggest gaming market, so developers take its product ratings very seriously. Of the 1,791 games rated by the American Entertainment Software Rating Board (ESRB) in 2009:

**60%** received an E (Everyone) rating
**16%** received an E10+ (Everyone 10+) rating
**18%** received a T (Teen) rating
 **6%** received an M (Mature) rating for adults only

## No small task

More than 1,000 employees worked on *Grand Theft Auto 4*. Tasks ranged from studying New York traffic patterns for realism to contacting more than 2,000 people to secure the rights to the music that makes up the soundtrack. The game took three-and-a-half years to make and cost around $100 million.

**The design doc** 2
A comprehensive design document is put together, containing the core game details, features, and deadlines. Games can spend a long time in development. Maxis's 2008 game *Spore* took nine years.

**The storyboard** 3
The characters, worlds, scenes, and endings are sketched out and, later, scripted and graphics-choreographed.

**The pitch** 1
At meetings, meetings, and more meetings, the developer (the company that will construct the game) pitches its idea to the publisher (the company that will market the finished game).

**Engines and coding** 4
The game engine is the core software that handles how 3-D graphics are rendered onscreen. Many games use off-the-shelf engines, but that still leaves thousands of lines of program code to be written.

### Did you know?

*Call of Duty: Black Ops* broke the record for biggest-ever first-day game sales when it launched in 2010. A staggering 5.6 million copies were bought in the United States and Britain, worth around $360 million.

**Testing** 8
Like any software, the game is tested rigorously at various stages. The team spends thousands of hours checking for bugs.

**Launch** 9
Well before the release date, playable demos appear online or on DVDs included with magazines. Big games may be launched at celebrity-studded parties.

**Sound and voices** 7
The soundtrack is planned to fit the game, then composed and recorded (or the rights secured). Voice actors—sometimes even Hollywood stars—may record thousands of words of dialogue.

**Motion-capture technology** 6
Animation can be more realistic if it is based on real body movements. Actors wear suits covered in joint sensors, as high-speed digital video cameras record their movements frame by frame.

**Did you know?**
Game text and speech are translated and recorded to facilitate release in different countries. Some game graphics or particular scenes may be adjusted or deleted to fit in with the laws or culture of a particular country.

**Next steps** 12
Executives meet to review how the whole production went. If sales are high, the publishers may commission a sequel—and the whole process begins again!

**In stores** 10
At last! The game goes on sale amid a fanfare of promotion and advertising on TV, the Web, and social media. First week sales create a buzz and can make or break a game.

**Character building**
Artists develop how the scenes, objects, and characters will look. Game characters begin as sketches, then 3-D wire-frame models of their bodies are made on-screen, with layers and colors added on top.

**Two-way street** 11
The gaming community helps promote the game through social networking and reviews. If bugs or glitches are found, the developers may offer fixes or patches.

## Simulations

A sim is a game that allows you to simulate an activity. These range from virtual pet games to flight simulators and sports management games. Others simulate life evolving over several generations, or let you build a virtual home, town, or world. With more than 90 million units sold, *The Sims* is the biggest-selling simulation series ever.

## Racing games

Racing sped out of the arcades into homes on consoles and computers and is popular with all ages. Games such as *Forza Motorsport*, *SBK-09*, and the *Gran Turismo* series pride themselves on racing realism, using accurate models of vehicles and famous race circuits. Others, such as *Mario Kart* and *Konami Krazy Racers*, are more fantasy-based.

## Platform games

In the 1980s and early '90s, about a fifth of all games sold were platform games, featuring characters that leap between suspended platforms or over obstacles in different scenes. From *Jet Set Willy* and *Donkey Kong* to various Sonic and Mario games, including *Super Mario 64* with its 3-D game play, platforms are especially popular on handheld consoles.

## Role-playing games

Known as RPGs, these complex games prove highly addictive to loyal gamers, who generally control a group, or party, of characters on various quests. Most RPGs are set in fantasy worlds or sci-fi settings. Online RPGs with huge followings, such as *World of Warcraft*, are known as MMORPGs—massively multiplayer online role-playing games.

## Competitive sports

Many new consoles launch with free sports titles to attract buyers. From basketball to big bass fishing, these games are hugely popular, particularly with casual gamers. Many top games feature real-life sporting champions. The top-selling sports game franchise to date is the *EA Sports FIFA* series, which has sold more than 65 million copies.

## Puzzles and quizzes

SCORE: 10

LEVEL 2

TETRIS

Games that challenge and train your brain come in a range of formats, from online and handheld trivia quizzes to graphic puzzles and cryptic word games. Not one is more famous than Alexey Pajitnov's 1984 creation, *Tetris*. More than 100 million copies of the falling-blocks puzzle game have been sold for mobile phones alone since 2005.

## Third-person shooters

From *Space Invaders* onward, gamers have loved third-person shooters, in which they control a character moving through a game world in the near distance. This figure interacts with objects or other characters and, of course, fires all kinds of weapons. Enemies may range from plague-infested zombies (*Resident Evil*) to armed aliens (*Gears of War*).

## Games of strategy

Strategy games are usually turn-based, tactical games between two players or between one player and the computer. They include board games such as chess, war games such as *Command & Conquer* and *Total War*, and the legendary *Civilization* series, which includes *Civilization V* for PCs and the Internet MMORPG *Civilization World*.

# What do you want to play?

Like a shape-shifting monster in a sci-fi world, game types keep changing and evolving. In the distant past, they fell into just two types: slow-moving strategy or adventure games, and arcade games requiring quick reactions. Now games are incredibly involved and complex. *Gran Turismo 4*, for instance, has 721 cars available to customize and drive. Today there are many different game genres. Here are a dozen of the most popular types.

## Adventure games

Beginning with text-only games in the 1970s, adventures place the gamer in a world to explore. They involve meeting characters, collecting clues and objects, solving puzzles, and finding new places. Gently paced, early adventures such as *Zork* attracted new players to gaming. Compelling games such as *Myst* and *Fahrenheit* have kept the genre going.

## First-person shooters

These shooting games place you right in the action, looking at the game world through your character's eyes. They got a massive boost with the arrival of 3-D graphics in games such as *Wolfenstein 3-D* and *Doom*. Some games, such as *Halo: Reach*, have detailed stories and such high levels of graphic violence that they have an adult-only rating.

## Fighting

In the 1980s, most fighting games were beat-'em-ups, in which a character had to punch, kick, and knock out swarms of opponents. The release of *Street Fighter II* in 1991 saw a shift toward one-on-one fighting, continued by *Mortal Kombat*, *Virtua Fighter*, and *Tekken*. Pressing multiple buttons at high speeds produces a range of martial-arts-inspired moves.

## Got rhythm?

First seen in Japanese arcades, dancing games such as *Dance Dance Revolution* and *Pump It Up* test a player's rhythm and timing as they try to copy on-screen dance moves. They were followed by games allowing players to show off their musical skills, including *Guitar Hero* and the unusual *Donkey Konga*, which has a pair of bongos as the game controller.

## Did you know?

In September 2002, Faiz Chopdat became the first British citizen to be jailed for playing *Tetris* on his mobile phone on an aircraft. This is against the law because it could interfere with communications

# Console wars

A battle is raging for world supremacy. To the victor goes untold millions, make that billions, of dollars and dominance. To the loser may go defeat, large losses, and a retreat from the game console arena. Welcome to the console wars—a fierce competition for increased market share between game machines. At the start of 2011, it's a seventh-generation, head-to-head battle between Microsoft's Xbox 360, Sony's PlayStation 3, and Nintendo's Wii.

## Did you know?

For much of the 1990s, Sega was a key player in the console wars. However, several poor-selling machines in a row saw the home of Sonic the Hedgehog move out of consoles and into computer software by 2001.

## Spectrum vs. C64

One of the first game wars occured in the UK in the 1980s between the Sinclair Spectrum and Commodore C64 computers. Millions of games were sold for both machines.

## Homegrown

Although the Wii is the best-selling machine in the Americas, with nearly half the market share, the homegrown Xbox 360 also does well, generating nearly 59 percent of total Xbox sales.

**45.3%**

**33.9%**

**20.8%**

## Most ever?

The PS2, first released in 2000, is the most successful console of all time with more than 140 million sold. It is still going strong. In 2010, Sony launched an HD television with a built-in PS2.

## Who's winning where?

Consoles have varying popularity in different regions for several reasons. Sony, for example, publishes many games that have been historically tailored to the Japanese market, whereas the types of games typically played by Westerners are more popular on the Xbox. As for the Wii, it's popular everywhere!

| Sony PlayStation 3 | 46.99 million worldwide |
| Nintendo Wii | 84.48 million worldwide |
| Microsoft Xbox 360 | 51.15 million worldwide |

## Americas

While Brazil and Mexico are growing national markets, the United States is where the big money is to be had. In 2008, the U.S. game industry was worth more than $11.7 billion of revenue—equal to 195 million copies of *Call of Duty: Black Ops* or 3.3 million PS3 consoles.

# Wii world conquest

At the moment the Wii is winning. It's the biggest-selling console in each region and makes up nearly half of all consoles sold worldwide. That's a big turnaround from 2002 when Nintendo's GameCube slumped a distant third behind the original Xbox and PlayStation. The secret? The Wii's mix of innovative, motion-sensing controllers and family titles that attract gamers of all ages. But it's not over yet. In 2010, both Sony with Move and Microsoft with Kinect (see page 90) launched motion-sensing competitors.

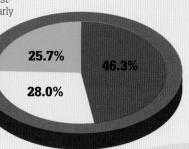

25.7%

46.3%

28.0%

| PlayStation 3 | Wii | Xbox 360 |
| --- | --- | --- |
|  |  | |
| $500–$600 million | $49-$149 million | $1.2 billion |

# Online revenue

Console manufacturers are making more and more money from online services, such as downloadable content, upgrades, in-game items, and subscription services. Microsoft leads the way with its Xbox Live subscription, which as of 2011 had more than 30 million members.

**In your hands**
Nintendo's handheld console family, the DS, is the undisputed handheld champion. More than 135 million DSs have been sold, including 32 million in Japan and more than nine million in the UK.

43.9%

29.9%

26.2%

**Popular choice**
More PlayStation 3s are sold in the EMEAA region than anywhere else, especially in Europe. By the summer of 2010, more than 16 million PlayStations had been bought in Europe.

**Big in Japan**
Japan is the second-largest market for games. Despite a reported nine percent drop in revenue in 2010, the Japanese market was valued at around $5.9 billion.

59.7%

32.7%

7.6%

# EMEAA

Europe, the Middle East, Africa, and Asia (minus Japan) make up the EMEAA sales region. Its eager gamers are responsible for 40 percent of worldwide Wii, PS3, and Xbox 360 sales. No major consoles are made in the EMEAA, but plenty of games are developed by companies from these areas.

N

# Japan

With two of the top three consoles designed in Japan, it's no surprise that the third, the Xbox, struggles to compete in this market. Sony and Nintendo duel both in the main console market and in a separate handheld battle between the DS family and Sony's Playstation Portable (PSP).

# Virtual worlds

Role-playing games (RPGs) have been popular ever since computers were first networked together. Controlling their characters, players take part in a story, quest, or adventure set in a virtual world. Players must make hundreds of decisions as they interact with other players, as well as game characters not controlled by players. The largest RPG games, Massively Multiplayer Online Role-Playing Games (MMORPGs), are hugely popular, with millions of participants.

## MUD

In **1978**, *MUD*, short for **"Multi-User Dungeon"** went online. It is considered the first multiplayer online game. *MUD* was a text adventure game in which users picked up points for collecting treasure and dropping it into a swamp, or for killing other players. Despite access to the game being rare in the early eighties, by 1984, more than **20,000 playing hours** had been notched up in *MUD*.

## Kesmai

In 1985, a multiplayer online game called ***Island of Kesmai*** was launched, a forerunner of today's MMORPGs. Players had to pay **$12 per hour** for connection to the game. *Island of Kesmai* supported up to 100 users playing at the same time. Today, *World of Warcraft* can have more than **a million people playing at one time**.

 **Lives**

## Runescape

With more than **10 million active users**, *Runescape* is the world's largest free MMORPG. It began in 2001, developed by two brothers, Andrew and Paul Gower, and was initially run from their parents' house in Nottingham, England. *Runescape* players chat, trade, and go on quests or enter different types of combat with other players. Now run by Jagex, up to **340,000 people** can enter the fantasy world of Gielinor and play simultaneously.

## Hattrick

RPGs are not all about slaying warlocks or battling alien hordes. Hattrick is a soccer management MMORPG in which players buy and sell players, and employ a range of tactics as they try to outsmart other teams. Launched in Sweden in 1997, it had more than **800,000 players** by 2010.

### NetEase

Many games charge a subscription to play, which means serious money. Chinese company NetEase, current operator of *World of Warcraft* in China, received **$1.59 billion** in online game revenues in three months in 2009.

## Second Life

Launched by the company Linden Lab in 2003, *Second Life* is an MMORPG with its own economy and three land masses to travel between.

*Second Life* players can own land, build their own objects from cubes, and even start their own businesses. In 2006, Ailen Greff (as her *Second Life* character Anshe Chung) became the first virtual millionaire, mainly through buying and selling land inside *Second Life*.

Goods and services in *Second Life* are paid for in Linden dollars, which can be bought using real dollars. In 2010, **L$255** equalled one dollar.

## $295

The price a premium member of *Second Life* needs to buy their first 705,000 sq ft (65,536 sq m) plot of virtual land is $295.

## 28,274,505

The number of hours players spent in *Second Life* during the month of January 2008.

## 481 million hours

The number of hours people spent inside the world of *Second Life* in 2009.

# World of Warcraft

The biggest MMORPG on the planet is *World of Warcraft (WoW)*, a fantasy role-playing game with more than 60% of the total number of MMORPG gamers. In 2010, more than **12 million gamers** paid a subscription to play *WoW*.

## WoW in numbers

**1,400+**
Locations to travel to

**1,000+**
Spells and skills to master

**700**
Different swords to wield

**150**
Books within the game to collect and read

**5,300**
NPCs (nonplayer characters)

**12,000**
Types of beasts and enemies to slay or flee from

### WoW players by continent in 2010

**22%** North America
**17%** Europe
**48%** Asia
**13%** Other

### One in five *World of Warcraft* players is female.

**20,000**
The number of computer systems running around 5.5 million lines of code that make *WoW* possible.

**3.3 million**
The number of copies of PC game *WoW: Cataclysm* sold on its first day of release in 2010—the fastest-selling PC game of all time.

**4,600**
The number of employees that work on *World of Warcraft*.

**BIG WINNERS**
*World of Warcraft* now runs online tournaments with cash prizes for the victors. At the 2010 *WoW* Global Arena tournament, there was prize money of **$200,000**, with **$75,000** going to the winner.

Score: 128895

## Gaming addiction

● With their ever-changing worlds and evolving characters, MMORPG gamers can get over-absorbed in the experience. For some, the games can prove seriously addictive. Treatment centers for game addicts have opened in China, South Korea, the Netherlands, and the United States.

● In 2006, a law was introduced in China limiting online gamers under the age of 18 to three hours of continuous play at a time.

● South Korean MMORPG addict Seungseob Lee, died in 2005 after playing *Starcraft* in an Internet café without rest for more than 40 hours.

# Video games arrive

Computer technicians wrote primitive versions of chess and checkers in the 1950s, but it wasn't until the 1970s that gaming took off. Video-game fans mainly hung out in arcades, but gaming was also possible at home on computers and game consoles. Since then, each new generation of console has brought better graphics and amazing new games.

**↓ 1974**
Game company Atari releases a home version of *Pong* and the first arcade racing game, *Gran Trak 10*.

**↓ 1980**
*Pac-Man* arrives in arcades, courtesy of the Japanese company Namco. It is the first video game with a named, animated hero and becomes hugely popular with female as well as male gamers.

**1984**
While working at Moscow's Dorodnicyn Computing Centre, Alexey Pajitnov creates *Tetris*. The falling puzzle-block game is a huge success, helping launch the Game Boy and selling 100 million copies for mobile phones alone.

**1961**
Students at MIT write the program code for *Spacewar!*— the first computer action game, featuring two battling spaceships. It runs the following year on a computer costing more than $120,000.

**↓ 1977**
Atari launches the 2600, its first games console, and the first to use cartridges.

**1982**
Microsoft releases *Flight Simulator 1.0*, taking the quality and graphics for such games to new levels.

**↓ 1988**
The Sega Genesis (called the Sega Mega Drive outside North America) is released.

**1952**
British computer scientist A.S. Douglas produces *OXO*, a simple tic-tac-toe computer game, at Cambridge University.

**1975**
American computer programmer William Crowther writes *Colossal Cave Adventure*, the first text adventure game for computers.

**↓ 1981**
A vintage year for classic games, 1981 saw the arrivals of *Donkey Kong* and the Mario character (known as Jumpman). Mario has since appeared in 116 different computer games—the most by a single character.

**1987**
The very first *Final Fantasy* game debuts in Japan. The *Final Fantasy* series will popularize graphic role-playing games.

**↑ 1989**
Nintendo launches its first Game Boy. This, and the late color version, will together s[e] more than 118 million units and have hundreds of differe[nt] games designed for them.

**↑ 1972**
The world's first home gaming console, the Magnavox Odyssey, originally designed by American inventor Ralph Baer in the late 1960s, goes on sale.

**↑ 1978**
*Space Invaders* debuts in Japan's arcades. Its addictive game play and high-score feature make it a major hit.

**↑ 1983**
The Nintendo Entertainment System (NES) range of game consoles begins production in Japan. Hugely influential, the consoles are manufactured for the next 20 years.

**1989**
Game designer Will Wright creates the city-building simulation game *Sim City*. Wright will go on to create a whole series of related games.

# 3-D master

Graphics in games remained blocky and flat until the arrival of 3-D gaming. One of the key people responsible was John D. Carmack, cofounder of id Software. Lead programmer on such groundbreaking games as *Wolfenstein 3D* and the *Doom* and *Quake* series, Carmack pioneered techniques to render graphics more quickly and make scenes more realistic, popularizing first-person shooters. His game engines have also been used on titles such as *Call of Duty* and *Half-Life*.

> "There are a lot of people [in the gaming industry] because they love games… Graphics and games are probably the most generally rewarding area of programming."
>
> **John D. Carmack**, 2000, American game programmer

**1993**
The American id Software releases *Doom,* a first-person shooter set in a fully 3-D environment, containing graphic violence. The game becomes both controversial and phenomenally popular.

**↓ 1999**
Sega launches its final console, the Dreamcast. It is discontinued just two years later.

**↑ 2004**
Nintendo release a handheld console, the DS. A month later, Sony's PlayStation Portable (PSP) (above) is released in Japan, launching in the United States and Europe the following year.

**→ 2010**
The Kinect motion-sensing device for Xbox 360 offers controller-free gaming on some titles, operated by the player's body movements and voice commands.

**1991**
The Japanese company Sega releases *Sonic the Hedgehog* and adopts the game's hedgehog hero as its company mascot.

**→ 1996**
Lara Croft stars in the original *Tomb Raider* game for the PlayStation.

**2004**
*World of Warcraft* debuts and becomes the world's most-played MMORPG.

**2007**
On its first day of release in the United States, the Xbox 360 game *Halo 3* generates $170 million in sales.

**↑ 1994**
Japanese company Sony launches its first PlayStation—a console that uses CDs instead of cartridges.

**1997**
Fantasy game *Ultima Online* debuts—the first of the MMORPGs (massively multiplayer online role-playing games). It attracts more than 100,000 paid subscribers in less than 6 months.

**↑ 2001**
The American company Microsoft enters the game-console market with the Xbox, the first major console to contain an internal hard drive.

**→ 2006**
Sony releases the PS3 console as a rival to the recently released Xbox 360.

**1992**
*Virtua Racing,* released on Sega arcade consoles and later on home machines, offers exciting 3-D graphics viewable from different angles, as well as a force-feedback steering wheel, which handles like a real one.

**1994**
With violence in some games rising, the Entertainment Software Rating Board (ESRB) is established in North America to give ratings based on content.

**1997**
*Final Fantasy VII* is released to rave reviews. The quality of its graphics sets new standards for game design.

**← 2006**
Nintendo introduces the Wii. With its motion-sensitive Wii remote and multiplayer games, it attracts millions of new casual gamers.

# Digital camera

Digital cameras focus light through a lens onto an electronic image sensor made up of a grid of thousands of microscopic photosites. These convert the light energy into electrical energy, which is processed inside the camera's electronics to produce an image that you can save to memory, and later print, e-mail, or upload to a photo-sharing site.

## Canon EOS 5D

This high-quality digital SLR (single lens reflex), designed for serious photographers, stores its photos on CompactFlash memory cards. Its image sensor can capture images with a resolution of up to 4,368 x 2,912 pixels.

Top

Back

Eyecup

Mode dial to select shooting modes

1

2

3

4

5

Playback button to review pictures

CMOS sensor

LCD settings panel

Main dial to adjust settings

Battery compartment

Lenses work together to focus image

Front lens collects light from scene

8

6

7

9

Mirror

Rechargeable battery

Battery flap

## CMOS sensor

The Canon EOS 5D uses a CMOS (complementary metal-oxide semiconductor) sensor to capture images. Light focused by the lens reaches the sensor's surface where it is converted into electrical signals and sent to the camera's image processor.

Lens

Image on sensor

### 1 Viewfinder
The viewfinder of an SLR camera obtains a through-the-lens view by using a mirror to direct the image from the lens up to the viewfinder. When an image is taken, the mirror flips up, allowing light to hit the sensor instead.

### 2 LCD display
Measuring 2.5 in (6 cm) diagonally, the rear LCD (liquid crystal display) screen is made up of around 230,000 pixels. It can display menu and setting options but also allows you to review pictures immediately after they are taken.

### 3 Mainboard
The camera's main board contains its image processors and associated control microchips. The DIGIC II image processor receives electrical signals from the sensor and processes them into an image that is saved to memory.

### 4 Hot shoe
This bracket accepts the base of an external mountable flash gun—used to produce a flash of additional light in time with the camera shutter opening to obtain a bright image in dark or low-light conditions.

### 5 Shutter release button
The camera's shutter opens and closes rapidly, allowing a precise amount of light in to hit the sensor. Slow shutter speeds create motion blur, while fast shutter speeds are used to capture and freeze motion.

### 6 Lens mount
The lens mount allows a lens to firmly click into place. It aligns electrical contracts from the camera and lens so that when camera is set to autofocus it can instruct the motors in the lens to turn to focus the image.

## Lens

This 50 mm lens is described as prime or fixed, meaning it cannot change how closely it views the scene. Zoom lenses, however, can zoom closer or farther away from the subject.

### 7 Focus mode switch
Powered by a motor, the lens can be focused automatically by the camera. For more creative control, the photographer can focus by hand after flipping the switch to manual.

### 8 Focusing ring
This control allows the photographer to focus the lens manually by turning the ring until the image looks sharp, either through the viewfinder or on the rear LCD screen.

### 9 Lens thread
A screw thread allows circular glass filters to be screwed onto the front of the lens. Filters protect the lens and can enhance images by letting more or less of particular frequencies of light in.

# Digital photography

Before the arrival of digital cameras, most cameras used a strip of chemically coated film that reacted with light to create a photograph. Digital cameras have since taken over, built into everything from children's toys and mobile phones to the high-quality SLR (single-lens reflex) cameras used by professional photographers. For many, the best feature of digital photography is that images can be manipulated and transmitted via the Internet.

## ↗ Image storage

The most popular film format was 35 mm, which came in rolls of 12 to 39 exposures (images). Digital cameras store photos as image files, usually on memory cards. A 4-GB Secure Digital (SD) card, a common size, can hold more than 1,000 images. The largest SD cards, at 2 terabytes, are 512 times larger.

## ↗ The digital darkroom

Film photographers developed their images in light-free darkrooms. Serious digital photographers use their computers as darkrooms. Photo-imaging software can alter lighting, remove blemishes, and apply effects. Then, the final image is printed out on a photo-quality printer.

### In-camera editing

Many digital cameras allow users to edit and alter an image while it is still held in the camera's memory. This can involve changing the color or exposure level, cropping in close, or applying special effects filters— for example, to transform a color photo into a sepia one or apply a texture like that of a painting.

A morphing filter pulls the image out of shape.

A color filter gives the image a red tint.

A mosaic filter breaks the image up into small tiles.

### Quality photographs

Digital cameras give more control. Users can determine the quality and file size of their images and delete pictures they don't like. The quality of the final image depends on various factors, including the camera's image-sensor resolution, often measured in megapixels (millions of pixels), and the quality of the lens. However, as with film photography, the most crucial ingredient is the skill of the person taking the picture.

### Did you know?

An increasing number of digital cameras have built-in Wi-Fi. Users can upload their snapshots to a website straight from the camera.

2208 43'

### Digital images online

Stored as computer files, digital images are easy to e-mail to others or upload onto the Internet. Online apps allow users to play with their photos, turning them into game avatars or personalized greeting cards. Photographers can sell their images through online image libraries or share them on photo sites, such as Flickr, Snapfish, Picasa, and Photobucket.

**flickr**

Search    Photos   Groups   People

Everyone's uploads   Giraffe    Search

"The idea that an inventor can come up with some brilliant idea and somebody else will make it all happen is nonsense. If the idea is good enough, it's going to appear pretty crazy to almost everybody. Either you do it yourself or it ain't going to happen."

**Did you know?**

At the age of 12, Sinclair designed an underwater submarine, and at 19 his IQ was measured at 159 (genius level). He was president of British Mensa, the high-IQ society, from 1980 to 1997.

# Clive Sinclair

Fascinated with shrinking technology and making it more affordable, English inventor Sir Clive Sinclair (born 1940) developed matchbox-sized radios, pocket TVs, pioneering digital watches, and, in 1972, the world's first pocket calculator. In 1980, he introduced the world's smallest, cheapest computer, the ZX80, followed by the best-selling ZX81 and Spectrum home computers. Despite the failure of his C5 electric vehicle, Sinclair continued to invent unusual vehicles, including tiny folding bikes and the SeaScooter underwater transporter.

# Wired cities

While some parts of the world struggle for Internet access and remain on the wrong side of the digital divide, others are thriving. Their governments and industries have invested heavily to provide fast, plentiful, and free (or relatively cheap) broadband, Wi-Fi hotspots, and strong mobile phone links. There are plans to help people get the very most out of the available technology. In the world's most wired cities, information is never more than a mouse click or a touchscreen tap away.

## Seoul, South Korea

Seoul is the world's most wired city. More than 93 percent of its households have broadband. In many countries, broadband runs at 10–50 megabits per second (Mbps). By 2012, Seoul's broadband will run at 1,000 Mbps. The city is home to electronics giant Samsung. Other companies at the cutting edge of technology, including Microsoft, Nokia, and Cisco, use Seoul as a living laboratory, testing many new products there before releasing them worldwide.

**Always in touch**
A girl uses the touchscreen of an Irobi personal robot in a Seoul department store. South Korea is home to many manufacturers of high-tech products. Its capital was the first city in the world to run a Digital Mobile Broadcasting (DMB) plan, bringing TV stations and other services direct to mobile phones.

## Did you know?

Seoul plans to become even more wired. Its Ubiquitous Seoul or U-City project plans to link everyone and everything electronically. Computer networks will control the appliances in smart apartments, while smart cards will track individual travelers via radio waves.

## Tallinn, Estonia

The capital of Estonia is a beautiful medieval city, which just happens to be one of the most wired in Europe. Every seat in the parliament and town hall features a laptop, most bank transactions are performed online, and Estonians pay for travel tickets and parking fines using their mobile phones.

## Seattle, Washington

The northern seaport of Seattle is home to Microsoft, Amazon, the enormous digital picture library Getty Images, and a host of other high-tech companies. The city boasts powerful broadband access, which is provided free to local community groups, as well as Wi-Fi on buses and in parks.

A number of different types of signals can now be used to control appliances remotely, from infrared for your television remote, to Bluetooth on mobile phones and some laptops. Exciting applications are now applying remote control over long distances. They use the Internet to carry commands and deliver them to personal robots and other Wi-Fi–enabled devices.

**→ Remote robot**
This WowWee Rovio mobile webcam relies on Wi-Fi. It can send images to and be controlled by users anywhere in the world as long as they have an Internet-enabled device.

# Interacting with new technology

Technology is changing all around us and the old ways of controlling it may have to move aside. If even more technologies are to become part of our lives, and work seamlessly with us, devices and systems will need to offer simpler, more convenient, intuitive, and rewarding ways of interacting with them.

**← Radio control**
A child uses a radio transmitter to fly a glider. When the glider receives the signals sent out by the handheld transmitter, its electric motors move parts of the aircraft.

## RFIDs

Radio Frequency Identification (RFID) tags send a radio signal either constantly or when scanned. Warehouses and delivery firms use the tags for tracking. They are also attached to vehicles for toll roads and found in public-transportation smartcards. In Denmark's Legoland theme park, parents can rent RFID bracelets that track, alert, and locate children who get lost.

**← Taking dictation**
The latest speech-recognition software can generate almost error-free dictation. It recognizes spoken words and turns them into a text document in real time.

**→ The Xtag**
This electronic ankle tag uses RFID technology. It enables hospital employees to keep track of patients, particularly the young and elderly, who may not be able to say who they are.

## Voice power

Speech is natural, easy for most people to produce, and leaves the hands free for other tasks. The main challenges for voice-controlled technology are canceling out background noise and recognizing a massive spoken vocabulary. These are being overcome, and voice control is already being used for noncritical functions in vehicles, smartphones, computers, and game play.

**↑ Eurofighter *Typhoon***
Some planes allow a pilot to switch radar mode, control displays, and perform navigation tasks using voice commands.

**→ Immersive VR**
A research scientist at the Earth Simulator Center in Yokohama, Japan, explores a VR model of the Earth. VR is used in science to study complex structures from any viewpoint or angle.

**← The Ring Wall**
Located in Nurburg, Germany, this giant touch screen is bigger than 5,500 computer screens. It supports multi-touch gestures by up to 80 people at once.

**← Hands on**
Microsoft Surface embeds touch screens in tables and surfaces. Responsive to devices such as cameras, paintbrushes, and more than 50 simultaneous touches, they offer exciting possibilities.

# Touchscreens

The first touch sensor was developed in 1971. During their short history, touchscreens became the most natural way of controlling digital organizers in the 1990s, and then smartphones and tablets. What next? Large smart surfaces can now respond to many people's command gestures at the same time. They can also recognize an object placed on the surface, calling up information about the object.

**← Gesture sensing**
This man is trying to "catch" swirling pieces of paper on a Monster Media gesture-sensing device. Interactive screens like this are already being used for advertising.

# Gesture- and motion-sensing

These systems use cameras to capture and isolate a person's movements, then match them to similar moves in their memory to perform commands. For example, a swipe of the hand might turn a web page, and a flat palm facing forward might pause a program. Already popular in game consoles, such systems may soon work on mobile devices.

**→ Step on it**
Children play on a Reactrix StepScape interactive ad. As it senses movement, the ad changes its display to produce a simple game or activity.

# Virtual reality

VR places a person inside a computer-simulated environment that appears real to the senses. The virtual world is projected inside a head-mounted display (HMD) and interaction is possible via a controller fitted with sensors. VR is used by the military and in industry for teaching, engineering tasks, and testing new product design.

**↑ VR glasses**
The latest HMDs project fractionally different viewpoints into each eye, which the brain processes into a 3-D view. Sensors track the movement of the head and shift the view.

**→ Finding information**
An interactive screen at Tampa International Airport allows travelers to search for accommodation and transportation using gestures and a large touch screen.

# Supercomputers

You've been lucky enough to get a pass into China's National Supercomputing Center, based in the northern city of Tianjin. Supercomputers are the beasts that governments, universities, and industry use to tackle massive computing tasks. What stands before you, housed in 103 chilled cabinets, is the world's most powerful computer, the Tianhe-1A. It has more processing power than 175,000 top-of-the-line laptop PCs.

## Top of the flops

"Flops" (floating-point operations per second) are one way to measure a computer's performance. Home PCs can perform at thousands, even millions of flops, but the top supercomputers work in petaflops—a quadrillion calculations per second! The Tianhe-1A's peak speed is more than 2.5 petaflops.

## Did you know?

Computing power increases rapidly each year. The 1970s supercomputer Cray 1, designed by Seymour Cray (see right), was rated at around 100 megaflops—slower than an Xbox 360 or PS3 game console!

天河高效能计算机系统

## Big beast

The Tianhe-1A contains 14,336 Xeon X5670 processors and 7,168 Nvidia Tesla M2050 graphics cards. It cost around $88 million to build and costs an additional $20 million a year to run. Its jobs include modeling weather patterns and number-crunching for oil exploration.

## What do they do?

Supercomputers are often put to work modeling how galaxies move and collide (left), how major weather systems form and move, what happens to all the particles in a major explosion, or how atoms behave in a chemical reaction. All these tasks involve mind-numbing amounts of calculation that would take too long on regular computers—or even be impossible to do.

## In the past

One man, electrical engineer Seymour Cray, dominated supercomputer design for decades and continues in the field today. He worked on the world's first commercial supercomputer, 1964's CDC 6600, before forming his own company. Many of Cray's early designs, such as the 1984 X-MP/48 (above), were circular to help reduce the distance that processing signals had to travel.

> ## "The scientific research that is now possible with a system of this scale is almost without limits."
>
> Guangming Liu, chief of the National Supercomputer Center, China

## Machine perception

The process of seeing an object, recognizing what it is, and recalling stored information about it—a process called perception—comes naturally to humans. Researchers in the field of machine perception are trying create computers that can do this too. Machines have to use sensors, such as cameras, to "see" their surroundings, and then process and store the data to build up a model of the world.

**→ Robot marathon**
The first ever robot marathon in Osaka, Japan, in 2011 was won by a robot that used aspects of AI to follow the 42-km- (26-mile-) long course autonomously, without human intervention.

# Artificial intelligence

American artificial intelligence (AI) pioneer Marvin Minsky described AI as "the science of making machines do things that require intelligence if done by men." That is just one definition. AI draws on many subjects, from computing to psychology. At its cutting edge, it can involve creating machines that can compete with humans.

**↑ Nexi**
Robot Nexi is able to view and map the features on a human face to figure out what emotion it is showing. Then, in response, it puts a suitable expression on its own face.

**← Talk of the future**
Kurzweil is an inventor and pioneer of many technologies including music synthesizers and machines capable of speech. He believes that further boosts in computing power will lead to major advances in AI.

## Intelligent cars

AI research is working toward driverless vehicles (with no human remote control) that can navigate a route, obey traffic rules, and avoid obstacles. The cars must process information from cameras, laser range-finders, and other instruments. In 2007, the U.S. Department of Defense tested 11 driverless cars over a 60-mile (96 km) course that mimicked city streets. Six reached the end.

## The future

Despite AI's frustratingly slow progress, many people remain optimistic about its future. These include the inventor, author, and lecturer Ray Kurzweil. In 2010, he predicted that "Machines will follow a path that mirrors the evolution of humans. Ultimately, however, self-aware, self-improving machines will evolve beyond humans' ability to control or even understand them."

**→ Boss in action**
The winner of the Department of Defense's challenge was a vehicle called Boss. The prize was $2 million.

# Social learning

Researchers are developing machines that learn new tasks and skills by having them work alongside and interact with humans. Robots such as Leonardo bring us a step nearer to the goal of a truly intelligent machine. Instead of being programmed for every task, they build up understanding in the same way that humans do—by mimicking the actions and behavior of other humans.

↑ **Leonardo**
Fitted with a camera, the robot Leonardo is capable of recognizing and remembering faces it has seen before. It can also track objects that it is familiar with, moving its head to follow the object's path.

# What's on TV?

In 2011, the trivia quiz show *Jeopardy!* featured its first nonhuman contestant. The *Watson* program runs on a cluster of fast servers, contains a giant database of facts, and, most importantly, can understand slang and puns. Before buzzing to answer, *Watson* has to narrow down choices, make decisions, and build confidence in its answers by running thousands of checks and comparisons. It may revolutionize machine learning.

↑ **Quiz champion**
In February 2011 on its first network TV appearance, *Watson* defeated two former *Jeopardy!* champions, Brad Rutter and Ken Jennings.

# Playing chess

In 2006, Russian Vladimir Kramnik was the chess champion of the world. Then he took on a computer running the *Deep Fritz* chess program and lost 2–4. With its complex moves and strategy, chess has long been used as a test of machine intelligence. IBM's *Deep Blue* chess program, which defeated Russian grand master Garry Kasparov 2–1 in 1996, was able to analyze as many as 200 million different moves.

↓ **Kramnik vs.** *Deep Fritz*
Grand master Vladimir Kramnik considers his next move during his six-game contest against *Deep Fritz.* The chess tournament took place in Bonn, Germany, in December 2006.

# What makes a robot?

Robots inhabited science fiction movies and stories long before they became scientific fact. The first robots emerged in the 1960s and have since exploded in range, size, and versatility. Robots tend to perform humanlike actions but with greater precision, repetition, or force than we can ever manage, or in locations we cannot or dare not visit.

## Core components

Robots vary greatly in shape, form, and function, but most have similar key parts enabling them to work effectively and efficiently. The vast majority of robots rely on microprocessors and electronics.

### End effector

Many robots have parts called end effectors that interact with the environment or manipulate objects. An industrial robot arm, for example, can be fitted with different tools to perform a range of tasks.

### Controller

The controller is the processor or "brain" of the robot. It keeps all the parts of the robot working together and makes decisions based on feedback sent to it from the sensors.

### Sensors

Devices like touch detectors, GPS, cameras, and temperature sensors send data called feedback back to the controller. These sensors report the robot's condition and position.

### What is a robot?

A robot is an automated machine that can be programmed to perform a range of tasks, such as this industrial robot arm playing a game. A robot is able to react to events in its surroundings and make decisions. Some of its parts are capable of movement.

## Moving parts

Some robots may be fixed in place, but can move parts such as a jointed arm. Each direction that all or part of a robot can move in is called a degree of freedom.

## Drive system

Robots need power and systems to move their parts. Drive systems may use electric motors, or hydraulic systems using cylinders and pistons full of liquids.

## How many robots are there?

In November 2010, *IFR World Robotics* estimated that there were 8.6 million robots around the world. Many work in factories, while robotics researchers use challenges such as robotic soccer (below) to study how robots can share information and work together.

## What is autonomy?

Some robots can work for long periods without human intervention or guidance. There are autonomous robot submarines, for example, that can navigate away from rocks, icebergs, and other obstacles without any assistance.

## Why are robots useful?

Robots free us from having to perform many dull, unpleasant, or repetitive tasks in industry, such as welding, placing hot metal parts, and spray-painting. They can often work faster and for longer periods than people, performing tasks beyond our strength or accuracy.

## Military robots

In many countries the military has helped fund robotics research, as well as deploying robots for a range of tasks. In the air, unmanned aerial vehicles (UAVs) are used for surveillance of enemy locations. On the ground, robots patrol military compounds as security guards or move ahead of human troops, finding and disarming unexploded bombs and mines.

**→ Robot flyer**
This UAV, the MQ-1 Predator, can fly for up to 24 hours at a time. On-board imaging and other surveillance instruments spy on targets on the ground.

97-3034

**→ Bomb disposal**
A French military bomb-disposal robot approaches an unexploded car bomb. It will blast a jet of water into the bomb to disrupt its circuits.

# Types of robots

Robots come in all shapes and sizes, from the tiniest micro aerial vehicles to huge, heavy-lifters used in industry, construction, and space. These hard-working machines perform all kinds of dirty, dangerous, or boring tasks for us. They crawl through sewers, check chemical plants for toxic leaks, defuse bombs—and even flip burgers!

## Industrial robots

More than a million robots work in factories around the world. Automated Guided Vehicles (AGVs) transport materials from place to place, while high-speed robot arms work on production lines, assembling, spray-painting, and welding. A small but growing number of robots work in mining, demolition, and other industries.

**← Robo dog**
In 1999, the Sony AIBO thrilled owners with its ability to respond to speech commands in Spanish or English, take pictures with its cameras, and learn from its environment.

## Entertainers and educators

Robots displayed in museums or at events always fascinate and entertain. Building simple robots is a hands-on way to learn about mechanics, electronics, and computing, as well as robotics. With kits such as LEGO Mindstorms™, hobbyists can build, modify, and program their own machines.

**↑ Sony QRIO**
The singing, dancing QRIO humanoid robot, created in 2003, stood 24 in (60 cm) tall. It had 38 joints and "ran" at 9 in (23 cm) per second—fairly fast for a biped robot.

**← Demolition droids**
A Brokk demolition robot helps dismantle nuclear power station laboratory. Demolition robots can operate in high-risk environments, leaving human worker a safe distance away.

↖ **Learning with Cog**
MIT's Cog robot was built to learn more about how a robot can sense touch, adjust its grip, and coordinate its parts like a human.

## Research robots

Right now, robotics researchers are designing, testing, and perfecting new robots. Some of these robots are prototypes of machines that will eventually go out into the world—or even into space. Others will remain in the lab, helping researchers to perfect sensing or movement technologies, or to investigate how a robot can learn from experience or interact.

↑ **Robot rovers** So far, robots have only been able to travel very slowly on Mars. However, these robot explorer balls developed for NASA are light enough for Martian winds to blow them across the surface.

↖ **Production line pals**
At this Kia factory in Slovakia, industrial robots are spot-welding car chassis. The factory uses 410 robots to produce more than 200,000 vehicles a year.

← **Restaurant robot**
This is one of four Motoman robot waiters working in the Hajime Restaurant in Bangkok, Thailand. Diners can order their meal by touch screen.

→ **Fire bot**
The Japanese Guardrobo D1 can operate as a warehouse or office security guard. It patrols buildings, investigates disturbances, and can detect and extinguish fires.

## Service and security

Large numbers of robots work in service industries performing simple, repetitive tasks—cleaning skyscraper windows or airport concourse floors, mowing lawns, or ferrying supplies from place to place. Some even work directly with people as guides, waiters, security guards, and house sitters.

"Robots have been into the deepest oceans. They've been to Mars. They're just starting to come into your home. You could think of your living room as their Final Frontier."

# Cynthia Breazeal

Ever since seeing the first Star Wars film, Cynthia Breazeal (born 1967) has been fascinated by robotics. The author of the book Designing Sociable Robots, Breazeal is now director of the Personal Robots Group at the MIT Media Lab. She specializes in building robots such as Leonardo and Nexi that can interact with people and produce "emotional responses." Kismet (pictured), her most famous robot, reacts to human voices, movements, and expressions with speech, smiles, winks, and frowns of its own.

**Did you know?**

Breazeal built *Leonardo* with help from Stan Winston, the Oscar-winning special effects creator behind the monsters in *Aliens*, *Terminator*, *Predator*, *Jurassic Park*, and many other movies.

# Mars Rover

Landing on a cushion of giant air bags in January 2004 after a seven-month, 280-million-mile (450-million-km) journey, the Mars Exploration Rovers A and B (named *Spirit* and *Opportunity*) were designed to perform a 90-day mission. They far exceeded expectations and *Opportunity* is still roving around Mars in 2011.

**1 Twin pancams**
A pair of panoramic cameras on the rover's mast tilt and swivel around as they take high-resolution images of the robot's environment. These are processed together to form stunning 360-degree views of the Martian surface.

**2 Solar arrays**
The robot needs lots of electricity, which is provided by solar panels. They generate about 140 watts of power when fully lit up by the Sun. Rechargeable batteries store energy to keep the rover running overnight.

**3 Warm box**
The body holds its key electronics in a warmed box, because nighttime temperatures on Mars can drop to below -139°F (-95°C). The box holds the robot's computer, which runs at less than one hundredth the speed of a home PC.

**4 High-gain antenna**
For around three hours a day, the Earth and Mars are aligned in such a way that the robot can transmit and receive signals directly, swiveling the 12-in- (30-cm-) wide dish so it faces Earth.

Navigation camera

Mast raises 4.5 ft (1.4 m) above the ground

Spectrometer to identify and locate minerals

1

2

3

5

6

7

### 5 Mobility system
All six wheels are driven by electric motors with independent steering of both the front and rear pair. The wheels are mounted on a suspension system, allowing the robot to tilt severely without toppling, and to roll over rocks more than 8 in (20 cm) in diameter.

### 6 Microscopic imager
Mounted on the robot's jointed arm, this camera can take detailed images of soil and rock particles as small as 0.04 in (0.1 mm) across.

### 7 Rock abrasion tool
The rock abrasion tool is a tiny grinderlike device that rubs away small slivers of weathered Martian rock so that other instruments can work on the clean, pure rock below.

# How it moves
With radio signals taking 20 minutes to reach Mars, controlling a robot in real time is impossible. NASA's robot drivers plan the next day's movement as instructions, which are uploaded to the robot for the next day.

**Step 1**
The rover takes images of the terrain ahead using navigation cameras fitted to the mast. These images are analyzed to build up a 3-D picture of the ground ahead.

**Step 2**
From its photos and data, the robot rover builds a map that identifies obstacles to avoid and the areas that are safe to drive through. It can then plot the ideal path forward.

Low-gain radio antenna

4

Wheels have cleats to help grip loose ground

# Ongoing mission
*Opportunity* has traveled more than 87,600 ft (26,700 m) up and down craters and is still going. On its way, the robot and its twin, *Spirit*, have sent back thousands of images and measurements of Mars. The robots have also made crucial discoveries, including strong evidence that water once flowed on the surface of the planet.

**Top**

**Front**

# Robot hospital

Robots are at work in hospitals, performing a surprisingly varied range of tasks. If you find yourself in the hospital at some point in the future, chances are that some part of your stay will be assisted by robots. They might deliver your meals, prescribe your drugs, or return you to the ward from the operating room. Robots might even perform surgery on you—they are already involved in thousands of operations a year.

## ↗ Working from the inside

In the future, medical staff may send microscopic robots into patients' bodies, through cavities or tiny incisions. These tiny machines would be able to diagnose problems and fix them from the inside.

● Scientists hope that the microTec submarine (below, imagined inside a human artery), built up from layers of acrylic just 0.0004 in (0.001 mm) thick, might one day travel along blood vessels, repairing damage from within.

● In the distant future, even tinier nanorobots, built to the scale of atoms, might be injected into your body to fight diseased cells directly.

### Operating room
Robots such as the Da Vinci (see right) are becoming a more common sight in the operating room. Surgical assistants such as ROBODOC have carried out more than 24,000 knee or hip replacement operations, and can drill, cut, and grip with more accuracy than a human hand. Another robot, Neuromate, can even perform brain surgery.

### In the ward
Reducing the workload on orderlies and nursing staff, automated guided vehicles (AGVs) can fetch and carry blankets, food, and supplies, saving hundreds of working hours. Robots may soon assist with the direct care of patients, lifting people out of bed or alerting human medical staff if a patient falls.

### Robotic replacements
Advances in technology are improving the latest generations of replacement body parts, including artificial arms and legs. Packed with microprocessors and sensors, smart prosthetic limbs can adjust the amount of flex or stiffness in the joints, making it easier for the wearer to lift, bend, or walk.

### Behind the scenes
Support robots in hospitals do jobs such as cleaning floors and dispensing drugs. The Robot-Rx can handle a dozen prescriptions a minute as it scans bar codes and selects the right drug and dosage from the pharmacy. This robot dispenses around 500 million medications each year in U.S. hospitals.

## The HelpMate

Created by Joseph Engelberger (see page 135), HelpMates roll quietly around hospitals, ferrying drugs, blankets, meals, and other essentials. They use light direction and range (LIDAR) scanners to track light, determine direction, and figure out their distance from obstacles.

## CareBot and NurseBot

Researchers are working on prototype personal robotic companions to help care for the elderly. CareBot (left) and NurseBot could help patients with exercises, remind them to take medicine, raise the alarm in an emergency, and act as a link to the outside world.

## The DEKA Arm

Advanced prosthetic limbs can give an amputee almost the same range of movement as a human arm. The DEKA weighs around 8 lb (3.6 kg)—about the same as a woman's arm. It contains numerous microprocessors and compact electric motors to control movement.

## Da Vinci

Providing 3-D images from inside the body, this multi-armed robot works with pinpoint precision under the control of a human surgeon. More than 1,500 hospitals worldwide have one or more da Vincis, and these robots perform hundreds of thousands of operations a year.

## MySpoon

Designed by SECOM in Japan, the award-winning MySpoon arm helps the ill, disabled, or elderly at meal times by scooping up manageable portions of food and raising them to the person's mouth. Operated by a single push button, it can handle any food—from soup to spaghetti.

## First responders

Rescue robots can help at the scene of a disaster or accident. They can clamber over or through rubble to find victims using thermal-imaging cameras, and make contact with rescuers. They can also deliver life-saving oxygen, water, or medicine.

## Tmsuk Enryu

This powerful Japanese "rescue dragon" robot stands 11.5 ft (3.5 m) tall and can tear off car doors so that medical staff can reach victims trapped inside. Each of its twin robot arms is able to lift up to 1,100 lb (500 kg), making them strong enough to carry people to safety.

## Space

Airless, waterless, freezing-cold space is the ultimate challenge for exploration. Robots are usually sent on one-way missions never to return, but the results of their work—thousands of photographs and scientific readings—can be beamed back to Earth.

### Viking landers
In July 1976, after a 10-month journey through space, *Viking 1* landed on Mars. It was followed, about 6 weeks later, by *Viking 2*. The robots took the first color images of the planet's surface. Their arms picked up and analyzed soil samples, and then radioed the results back to Earth.

### Voyager 1
Launched in 1977, this long-distance space probe is still sending back data. *Voyager 1* is now in the outer reaches of the Solar System after a 13-billion-mile (22-billion km) journey past Jupiter, Saturn, Uranus, and Neptune.

### Canadarm2
Astronauts can ride on this giant robot arm attached to the International Space Station, in orbit 220 miles (350 km) above the Earth. *Canadarm2* is 57.7 ft (17.6 m) long and can handle payloads weighing up to 226,000 lb (116,000 kg).

### QinetiQ Zephyr
This solar-powered robot with a 74 ft (22.5 m) wingspan is designed to fly slowly, but for long periods, carrying out aerial photography or surveillance at low cost. In July 2010, it flew nonstop for a staggering 14 days and 21 minutes.

### Micro Aerial Vehicles (MAVs)
Still under development, MAVs are robot fliers, often no bigger than your hand, intended for local exploration, aerial photography, and police surveillance. One day, squadrons of MAVs may fly search-and-rescue missions.

### Global Hawk
This military Unmanned Aerial Vehicle (UAV) has a 116 ft (35.4 m) wingspan and is used to explore large areas of terrain in a single flight. Its onboard surveillance equipment includes high-resolution cameras and radar.

# Robot explorers

Robots make excellent explorers. They do not need the oxygen, water, and food that human explorers demand. Instead, they use batteries or fuel cells, or even generate their own energy from solar panels. Robots can also be sent on high-risk journeys with little or no hope of return. The toughest ones are built to withstand extremes, from the pressures of the ocean depths to the temperatures in space, which average a bitter -427 °F (-255 °C) but can reach hundreds of degrees.

## Sky

Flying robots have many uses. They are used to explore and map isolated areas, from remote forests to icy wastes, and to spy on enemy territory. The *Robofalcon* has a less impressive but no less important job—scaring bird flocks away from airport runways.

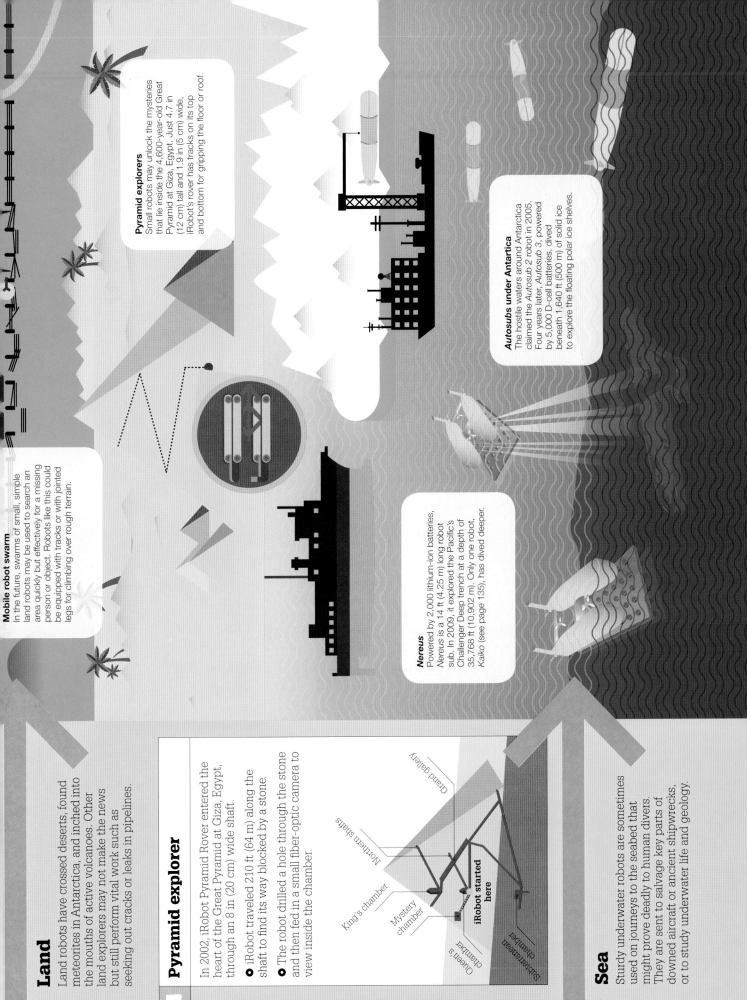

## Land

Land robots have crossed deserts, found meteorites in Antarctica, and inched into the mouths of active volcanoes. Other land explorers may not make the news but still perform vital work such as seeking out cracks or leaks in pipelines.

### Pyramid explorer

In 2002, iRobot Pyramid Rover entered the heart of the Great Pyramid at Giza, Egypt, through an 8 in (20 cm) wide shaft.

○ iRobot traveled 210 ft (64 m) along the shaft to find its way blocked by a stone.

○ The robot drilled a hole through the stone and then fed in a small fiber-optic camera to view inside the chamber.

Grand gallery

Northern shafts

King's chamber

Mystery chamber

**iRobot started here**

Queen's chamber

Subterranean chamber

## Sea

Sturdy underwater robots are sometimes used on journeys to the seabed that might prove deadly to human divers. They are sent to salvage key parts of downed aircraft or ancient shipwrecks, or to study underwater life and geology.

**Mobile robot swarm**
In the future, swarms of small, simple land robots may be used to search an area quickly but effectively for a missing person or object. Robots like this could be equipped with tracks or with jointed legs for climbing over rough terrain.

**Pyramid explorers**
Small robots may unlock the mysteries that lie inside the 4,600-year-old Great Pyramid at Giza, Egypt. Just 4.7 in (12 cm) tall and 1.9 in (5 cm) wide, iRobot's rover has tracks on its top and bottom for gripping the floor or roof.

*Autosubs under Antartica*
The hostile waters around Antarctica claimed the *Autosub 2* robot in 2005. Four years later, *Autosub 3*, powered by 5,000 D-cell batteries, dived beneath 1,640 ft (500 m) of solid ice to explore the floating polar ice shelves.

*Nereus*
Powered by 2,000 lithium-ion batteries, *Nereus* is a 14 ft (4.25 m) long robot sub. In 2009, it explored the Pacific's Challenger Deep trench at a depth of 35,768 ft (10,902 m). Only one robot, *Kaiko* (see page 135), has dived deeper.

# Advance of the robot

It all started with a squat box with an extended, jointed arm that handled red-hot metal castings in a car factory. Deployed in 1961, the Unimate was the world's first industrial robot, capable of learning 200 commands. Before then, gifted mechanical engineers had assembled machines that performed automated tasks… but nothing that matched the versatility of a true robot. Robotics is still in its infancy, but here are some of the milestones that have made it such an exciting field of research.

## Did you know?

In 2003, an Odyssey Marine Exploration underwater robot, *ZEUS*, helped recover more than 51,000 gold and silver coins from the 1865 shipwreck of the SS *Republic*.

---

**↘ 1801**
Joseph-Marie Jacquard invents the first programmable machine—a weaving loom in which the patterns are controlled by a series of cards with holes punched in them.

**↑ 1948**
Professor Norbert Weiner of the Massachusetts Institute of Technology (MIT) publishes his influential book *Cybernetics*. It looks at how communications and control work in animals, and how they might work in machines.

**↓ 1970–3**
A team at Waseda University, Japan, build Wabot-1, the first life-size humanoid robot. It has a pair of arms and legs, two cameras for simple eyes, but no head.

**1984**
The humanoid robot Wabot-2 is built at Waseda University. It reads sheet music through its camera eye and plays the organ with its 10 fingers and two feet.

**↑ 1966**
At the Stanford Research Institute, work begins on Shakey, the first autonomous moving robot able to navigate around obstacles. Its top speed is 6.5 ft (2 m) per hour.

**↑ 1976**
The *Viking 1* and *2* spacecraft land on Mars. Their robot arms are the first robots to reach another planet.

**c. 270 BCE**
Greek scholar Ctesibius of Alexandria designs pumps and water clocks with complex mechanisms.

**1938**
The first programmable spray-painting machine is designed for the DeVilbiss Company.

**1956**
Joe Engelberger and George Devol form the world's first robotics company, Unimation.

**1981**
Japanese scientist Takeo Kanade builds the first direct-drive robot arm, installing electric motors directly into the joints of the arm to make its movements faster and more accurate.

---

**↓ 1738**
French inventor Jacques de Vaucanson creates a mechanical duck that can mimic some of the actions of a real one.

**1920**
Czech playwright Karel Capek coins the term "robot" in his play *Rossum's Universal Robots*.

**↑ 1942**
Isaac Asimov writes a story about robots, *Runaround*, which contains his Three Laws of Robotics. He later adds a Zeroth Law. These laws have influenced robot development in real life as well as in books and movies.

**1959**
The Artificial Intelligence Laboratory at MIT is founded.

**1961**
The first Unimate robot begins work in the Trenton, New Jersey, General Motors factory. It puts in a 100,000-hour shift before retiring and going on display at the Smithsonian Museum.

**↑ 1970**
The Soviet Union's Lunokhod 1 moon rover becomes the first machine to move across the surface of a body other than Earth. The eight-wheeled rover travels more than 6 miles (10 km).

**↑ 1975**
The PUMA (Programmable Universal Machine for Assembly) industrial robot arm is invented.

**1986**
The Remotely Operated Vehicle (ROV) *Jason Junior* photographs the *Titanic* shipwreck on the Atlantic Ocean floor.

**↑ 1979**
The Stanford Cart autonomous robotic vehicle navigates a room of obstacles.

# Joseph F. Engelberger

Inspired by the sci-fi *I, Robot* stories of Isaac Asimov, Engelberger teamed up with engineer George Devol to form the world's first robotics company, Unimation, in 1956. Their robots inspired companies in Japan, Korea, and northern Europe. In the mid-1980s, Engelberger moved into service robots, producing a series of HelpMate robots for hospitals. Now in his eighties, Engelberger still lectures and writes on robotics.

> "Robot builders today have more technology available to them than has ever been used."

**Joe Engelberger,** 2003, in an interview with *Bloomberg Businessweek*

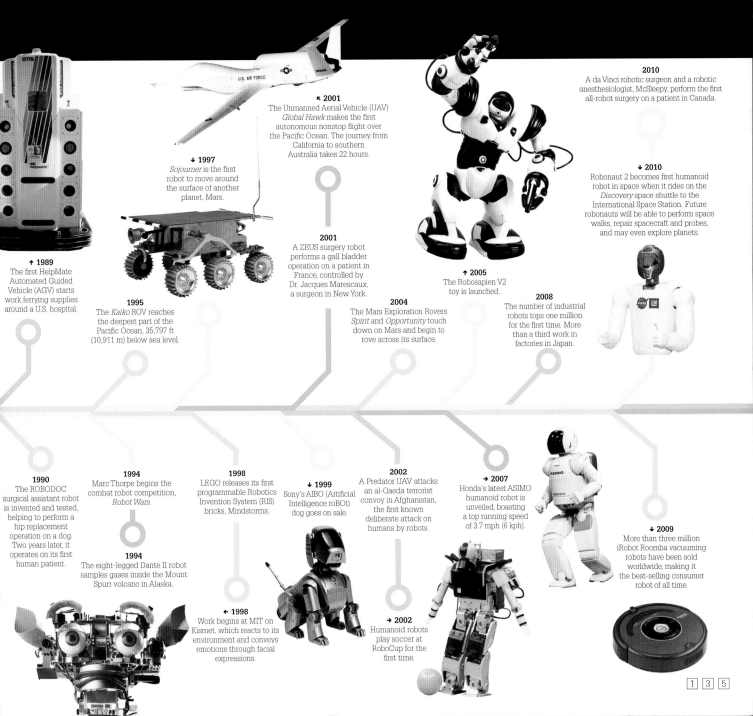

**↑ 1989**
The first HelpMate Automated Guided Vehicle (AGV) starts work ferrying supplies around a U.S. hospital.

**1995**
The *Kaiko* ROV reaches the deepest part of the Pacific Ocean, 35,797 ft (10,911 m) below sea level.

**↓ 1997**
*Sojourner* is the first robot to move around the surface of another planet, Mars.

**↖ 2001**
The Unmanned Aerial Vehicle (UAV) *Global Hawk* makes the first autonomous nonstop flight over the Pacific Ocean. The journey from California to southern Australia takes 22 hours.

**2001**
A ZEUS surgery robot performs a gall bladder operation on a patient in France, controlled by Dr. Jacques Marescaux, a surgeon in New York.

**2004**
The Mars Exploration Rovers *Spirit* and *Opportunity* touch down on Mars and begin to rove across its surface.

**↑ 2005**
The Robosapien V2 toy is launched.

**2008**
The number of industrial robots tops one million for the first time. More than a third work in factories in Japan.

**2010**
A da Vinci robotic surgeon and a robotic anesthesiologist, McSleepy, perform the first all-robot surgery on a patient in Canada.

**↓ 2010**
Robonaut 2 becomes first humanoid robot in space when it rides on the *Discovery* space shuttle to the International Space Station. Future robonauts will be able to perform space walks, repair spacecraft and probes, and may even explore planets.

**1990**
The ROBODOC surgical assistant robot is invented and tested, helping to perform a hip replacement operation on a dog. Two years later, it operates on its first human patient.

**1994**
Marc Thorpe begins the combat robot competition, *Robot Wars*.

**1994**
The eight-legged Dante II robot samples gases inside the Mount Spurr volcano in Alaska.

**1998**
LEGO releases its first programmable Robotics Invention System (RIS) bricks, Mindstorms.

**← 1998**
Work begins at MIT on Kismet, which reacts to its environment and conveys emotions through facial expressions.

**↓ 1999**
Sony's AIBO (Artificial Intelligence roBOt) dog goes on sale.

**2002**
A Predator UAV attacks an al-Qaeda terrorist convoy in Afghanistan, the first known deliberate attack on humans by robots.

**→ 2002**
Humanoid robots play soccer at RoboCup for the first time.

**→ 2007**
Honda's latest ASIMO humanoid robot is unveiled, boasting a top running speed of 3.7 mph (6 kph).

**↓ 2009**
More than three million iRobot Roomba vacuuming robots have been sold worldwide, making it the best-selling consumer robot of all time.

> *"There is no reason anyone would want a computer in their home."*
>
> **Ken Olsen**, cofounder and CEO of Digital Equipment Corp. (DEC), 1977

## Future promise

Scientists, businesspeople, and writers of the past promised us a future world of personal jet packs, frequent space travel, and cities in the sky. Technology has not delivered on these things yet. What people underestimated, however, was the rise of computing and the Internet.

# What next?

The worlds of computing, gadgets, gaming, and the Internet are constantly evolving. Some developments, such as personal robots or video phones, have been a long time coming. Others, such as the booming World Wide Web, were more sudden and took people by surprise. Predictions are always risky, but some key players have been confident enough to suggest what might be in store in both the near and more distant future.

> *"In 30 years, chores around the house will be a thing of the past. The robots will have evolved from automatic appliances to home automations systems."*
>
> **Helen Greiner**, cofounder of iRobot and The Droid Works robotics companies, 2009

## The pace of evolution

The speed of change is accelerating. It took thousands of years of human development before the invention of printing made it possible to spread knowledge widely, but less than 50 years to go from the first computers to the World Wide Web. Today, with a worldwide Internet-linked audience eager to adopt and adapt to new technologies, it is likely that change will happen even faster.

> *"They say a year in the Internet business is like a dog year… equivalent to seven years in a regular person's life. In other words, it's evolving faster and faster."*
>
> **Vinton Cerf**, Internet pioneer and, since 2005, a vice president of Google

### Thought control

One day you may be able to control gadgets and programs using only your brain and thought patterns. The field is in its infancy, but research is ongoing at many universities and at military and medical organizations. Several have already built headsets that measure brain activity and convert it into commands for appliances and games.

### Nanotechnology

Robots and machines built at "nano" scale are measured in nanometers, or millionths of millimeters. If nanotechnology becomes cheap and abundant enough, its impact could be enormous. Thousands of microscopic nanorobots could be sent to work inside machines and human bodies to repair any damage, while entire computer systems could be built on a pinhead.

### Smartware

Software is only going to get smarter and more personal, able to tailor itself to people's individual requirements and freeing them from a range of mundane tasks. Homes and domestic appliances are likely to be controllable over the Internet. Power supply, too, is going wireless. This demonstrator is showing off a "smart" kitchen counter. Just place special pans or toasters over a tiny "hotspot" and it is activated.

### Face-to-face phone calls

Video calls were often predicted or promised in the past but always led to disappointment. They are finally a reality. Apple's FaceTime is just the start. New-generation smartphones and tablets use cameras to stream live images over an Internet connection to enable face-to-face conversations. As the price of making such calls drops, new social networking sites based on real-time video links may boom.

### 3-D printers

Printers that can output 3-D objects are already here. They take thin, cross-section "slices" of a 3-D computer file and then print the slices. An additive material, such as melted nylon powder, builds up the 3-D object, layer upon layer. In the future, this amazing technology might make it possible to generate processors, entire circuit boards, and spare parts at home.

### The future of gaming

Gaming is likely to become even more diverse, with motion-sensing activities for casual gamers and increasingly immersive game worlds for dedicated gamers. Nonplayer characters equipped with AI will help populate virtual worlds and offer richer gaming experiences. Back in the real world, gaming competitions on TV may make celebrities of the world's leading players.

## Always-on networking

The future of Internet connectivity is all about more—more speed, power, and bandwidth, more availability, and more apps taking advantage of always-on Internet access. Increasing numbers of people will get Internet access. And as more become reliant on the Internet for work, education, information, and play, the pressures on its routers, servers, cables, and management will grow.

*"The future is really terrific and software is a big part of it... I am very optimistic we are really at a tipping point of some great stuff."*

**Nolan Bushnell**, Atari cofounder, 2010

# Glossary

### ARPANET
A pioneering computer network, founded in 1969, and considered the forerunner of the Internet. It was funded by the U.S.'s Advanced Research Project Agency (ARPA).

### Artificial Intelligence (AI)
The intelligence of machines. Also, the science and study of building machines that can learn and think in humanlike ways.

### authentication
The process of checking the identity of a user, program, or computer on the Web.

### avatar
A graphic figure that represents you on message boards, in chat rooms, and in 3-D virtual worlds.

### bandwidth (computing)
The maximum amount of data that can travel along a communications path, such as a cable, in a set time. It is often measured in kilobits or megabits per second.

### Bluetooth
A wireless system that uses radio waves to transmit data over short distances. It is used to allow communication between a mobile phone and its hands-free set, for example.

### broadband
Telecommunications systems in which a single cable can deliver a number of channels of data all at the same time and at high speed.

### browser
A computer program that allows people to find, view, and navigate between different websites or web pages.

### client
A computer that accesses a service or data on another computer via a network.

### e-book
A digital version of a printed book available in a file that can be sent via a network and read on a computer or e-reader device.

### fiber-optic cable
Cable made of thin strands of glass (or other transparent materials) that carries data over great distances in the form of pulses of light.

### game engine
A software system designed to build and run video games. Its tasks include creating graphics and moving objects in the game.

### gigabyte (GB)
1,000 megabytes. Hard disk drives are usually measured in GB capacity.

### GPS
Short for Global Positioning System, a means of navigation that uses a series of satellites orbiting Earth to give an accurate position on the Earth's surface.

### graphical user interface (GUI)
A system that lets users interact with their computer via small images called icons and a cursor, instead of typing in text.

### HTML
Short for hypertext markup language, a basic computer language used to format and provide links on text-based web pages.

### humanoid (robotics)
A robot that has human features, either in its appearance or its actions.

### hyperlink
A word, phrase, image, or icon on the World Wide Web that, if clicked, takes the user to a new document or web page.

### Internet
A global network made up of many networks, through which computers communicate by sending data in small units called packets. Each network consists of computers connected by cables or wireless links. The World Wide Web is accessed by means of the Internet.

### Local Area Network (LAN)
A network in which computers and other devices are connected together within a small physical area using cables or wireless links.

### mainframe
A large, powerful computer, often serving many connected terminals, and usually used by large, complex organizations.

### malware
Malicious software that can be transmitted to others by e-mail or downloads.

### microprocessor

A computer chip that contains most or all of the central processing unit (CPU) of a computer.

### MIT

The Massachusetts Institute of Technology, a leading center of computing, technology, and robotics research in the United States.

### nanotechnology

The science of building machines in sizes measured in nanometers. A nanometer is a millionth of a millimeter (0.00000004 in).

### open-source software

Free software that provides the source code so that advanced users can modify it.

### operating system

The program that manages a computer's resources. Its tasks include sending data to a screen and organizing files.

### pixel

Short for "picture element," a pixel is a tiny dot of light on a screen which together with thousands more make up the images on a display.

### random access memory (RAM)

Memory used by a computer to hold data that is currently in use and to perform operations on it. Data stored in RAM is usually lost when the machine is turned off.

### router

A device that routes data between different networks either via cable or wirelessly.

### sensor

A device that gives a robot or computer data about itself or its environment, such as temperature or location.

### server

A computer, or software on a computer, that provides services to other computers that connect to it via a network.

### SLR

Short for "single-lens reflex," a type of camera designed so that the user views the scene to be photographed through the lens of the camera. SLRs can be fitted with a range of lenses and can produce high quality images.

### sonar

A system that uses pulses of sound waves to detect solid objects or to measure distances.

### streaming

The ability to send music or video over the Internet as a continuous stream of data so that users can view or listen to it in real time, without waiting to download a complete file.

### tablet

A type of computing device that uses a touchscreen for input as well as display.

### TCP/IP

Short for "transmission control protocol/Internet protocol," a set of communications rules that control how data is transferred between computers on the Internet.

### torrent file

A way of greater sharing online in which parts of the file are downloaded from a number of servers. Each downloading user becomes a source for others who want the same file.

### touchscreen

An electronic device that responds to the touch of fingers or a stylus and can be used to input data or select options.

### uploading

The process of transferring data from one computer to another or from a storage device to a computer.

### virtual reality (VR)

A simulated, interactive 3-D environment, displayed in real time, used for education, entertainment, and product design.

### virus

A program that is capable of duplicating itself and infecting computers. Viruses vary from harmless nuisances to major security risks that can cripple computer systems.

### website

A group of related web pages that give information about a particular subject, company, or institution.

### Wide Area Network (WAN)

Computer networks that are connected together over long distances using telephone lines, fiber-optic cables, or satellite links.

### Wi-Fi

The technology that allows computers and other devices to communicate with each other using wireless signals.

### World Wide Web (WWW)

An interconnected set of hypertext documents spread throughout the Internet. The documents are formatted in HTML and kept on computers called servers.

# Index

# Credits

**DK would like to thank:**

Stefan Podhorodecki and June Chanpoomidole for help with design. Carron Brown, Victoria Hayworth-Dunne, and Jonathan Garbett for editorial help. Charlotte Webb for proofreading. John Searcy for Americanization. Jackie Brind for the index. Stefan Podhorodecki and Robert Scoble for photography. Roland Smithies for additional picture research.

**The author would like to thank:**

Steve Mersereau of Red Ink.

**The publisher would like to thank the following for their kind permission to reproduce their photographs:**

**8 Corbis:** Bettmann (cl). **8–9 Corbis:** Bettmann (c). **9 Getty Images:** Hulton Archive (tc). **Science Photo Library:** Nelson Morris (bc). **12 Computer History Museum:** Mark Richards (g). **Corbis:** Kim Kulish (h); Tetra Images (a). **Getty Images:** SSPL (c, d, f); The Bridgeman Art Library (b). **Image originally created by IBM Corporation:** (i). **Photolibrary:** Fotosearch Value (e). **13 Alamy Images:** imagebroker (e); John Joannides (k). **Associated Press AP:** Marcio Jose Sanchez (a). **Computer History Museum:** (b); Mark Richards (i). **© Intel Corporation:** (c). **Getty Images:** Phil Matt / Liaison (g); SSPL (d, f, j). **14–15 Getty Images:** Apic (c). **14 SRI International:** (cl). **15 Getty Images:** Hulton Archive (ca). **SRI International:** (tc, tr, br). **16 Alamy Images:** ClassicStock (bl). **Getty Images:** SSPL (tc). **Science Photo Library:** Martin Dohrn (b). **16–17 Corbis:** D&P Valenti / ClassicStock (c). **Getty Images:** SSPL (t, bc). **17 Alamy Images:** Ted Foxx (tr). **Corbis:** Lawrence Manning (br). **Getty Images:** Scott Davis / Department of Defense (DOD) / Time Life Pictures (crb). **18 Acer:** (tl). **19 Corbis:** Tim Pannell (br); Terry Why / Monsoon / Photolibrary (cr). **20–21 Corbis:** Ed Quinn. **20 Robert Scoble:** (cra). **21 Corbis:** Pallava Bagla (cr). **NCSA/University of Illinois:** (tl). **24–25 Getty Images:** David Clapp / Oxford Scientific. **25 Alamy Images:** Ron Niebrugge (tr). **www.subcom.com:** (cb). **27 Terremark Worldwide, Inc.:** SiliconValleyStock (tr). **Corbis:** Wu Kaixiang / Xinhua Press; Richard Nowitz / National Geographic Society (tl). **Getty Images:** Panoramic Images (b). **29 Alamy Images:** MTP (tr); TJP (clb). **Corbis:** Kim Kulish (cla). **Getty Images:** Ryan Anson / Bloomberg (crb); Gabriel Bouys / AFP (tl); Randi Lynn Beach / Bloomberg (bl); Tony Avelar / Bloomberg (br). **Symantec Corporation:** (cra). **32–33 Courtesy of Apple. 33 Corbis:** Bettmann (tl). **34–35 Corbis:** Terry W. Eggers. **36 Baidu Image Search Service:** (ca). **36–37 Seznam. cz, a.s.. :** (tc). **37 Corbis:** Peter Foley / Epa (tr). **38–39**

**Corbis:** Catherine Karnow (c). **© Google Inc. Used with permission:** (Google icons and logos). **38 Corbis:** Penni Gladstone / San Francisco Chronicle (bc). **39 Corbis:** Mario Anzuoni / Reuters (crb). **Getty Images:** Justin Sullivan (tc). **40–41 Bahnhof AB. 50 Getty Images:** Prakash Mathema / AFP (cb). **50–51 Getty Images:** Prakash Mathema / AFP. **51 Getty Images:** Prakash Mathema / AFP (tc). **Ncell :** (tr). **53 Corbis:** Ding Xiaochun / XinHua / Xinhua Press (tc). **61 Alamy Images:** Gary Lucken. **64 Corbis:** Nasa / Reuters (bl). **71 Getty Images:** Barcroft Media (crb); Toussaint Kluiters / AFP (tr). **Science Photo Library:** Bernhard Edmaier (cra). **72–73 © Google Inc. Used with permission:** Google Earth. **76 Corbis:** Justin Lane / Epa (h); Louie Psihoyos (c). **Fotolia:** ErickN (g); Julián Rovagnati (e); Seth (d). **Image originally created by IBM Corporation:** (f). **Twitter:** (e). **77 Adobe Systems Incorporated:** (c). **Amazon.com, Inc:** (f). **Courtesy of Apple:** (i). **Fotolia:** vectorsmartini (k). **Used with permission from Microsoft:** (g). **Mozilla:** (d). **Napster LLC:** (h). **youtube.com:** (j). **78 Alamy Images:** Art Directors & TRIP (bl). **Getty Images:** Maurice Ambler / Hulton Archive (tl). **Qidenus Technologies Gmbh:** (tr). **79 Alamy Images:** Asia Photopress (bl). **Corbis:** H. Armstrong Roberts (bc). **Getty Images:** Saul Loeb / AFP (br); Michael Ochs Archives (tl); Justin Sullivan (tr). **82–83 Corbis:** Atlantide Phototravel. **83 Getty Images:** Anne Frank Fonds / Anne Frank House (bl). **© Google Inc. Used with permission:** (c). **Science Photo Library:** Sam Ogden (tc). **84 Scott Beale / Laughing Squid:** (bl). **84–85 Corbis:** Roger Ressmeyer (bc). **85 Alamy Images:** Wendy White (tl). **Getty Images:** SSPL (cra, bc). **86–87 Alamy Images:** ArcadeImages. **86 Corbis:** Bettmann (cl). **87 Corbis:** HO / Reuters (tc). **90–91 Corbis:** Fred Prouser / Reuters. **Nintendo:** 90 **Getty Images:** ICHIRO / Photodisc (l). **Nintendo:** (c, crb). **91 Nintendo:** (cb). **93 Alamy Images:** Arterra Picture Library (tr). **94 Used with permission from Microsoft:** (tr). **103 Used with permission from Microsoft:** (ftr). **Nintendo:** (tr). **Sony Computer Entertainment America:** (tc). **106 Alamy Images:** ArcadeImages (br); Sinibomb Images (cla). **Dorling Kindersley:** (fcrb). **Lebrecht Music and Arts:** Interfoto (cl, bl). **Rex Features:** Peter Brooker (bc). **Wikipedia, The Free Encyclopedia:** (cr); Evan Amos (fbr). **107 Alamy Images:** Moviestore Collection Ltd (fcl); Hugh Threlfall (cr); Finnbarr Webster (clb); toy Alan King (cb); Tony Cordoza (bl); Lightly Salted (br). **Getty Images:** Urbano Delvalle (c); Albert L Ortega (tl); Hulton Archive (cl); Jordan Strauss (fcr). **110–111 Corbis:** Frans Lanting. **110 Photolibrary:** (bl). **SanDisk Corporation:** (cl). **114–115 Corbis:** Ocean. **114 Corbis:** Kim Kyung-Hoon / Reuters (c). **115 Corbis:** Benelux (tr); Bill Ross (cb). **116 Alamy Images:** Roderick Smith (crb). **Getty Images:** Ghislain & Marie David de Lossy (tl); Kent Smith /

First Light (clb); Yoshikazu Tsuno / AFP (br). **Rex Features:** Action Press (bc). **WowWee Group Limited:** (tr). **117 Corbis:** Ausloeser (bl); Robert Sorbo / Reuters (tl); Rick Wilking / Reuters (cla); Najlah Feanny (crb); Mcintyre, Scott / ZUMA Press (br). **SENSORY-MINDS GMBH:** (tr). **118–119 Corbis:** Imaginechina. **119 Science Photo Library:** David Parker (br); Daniel Price (tc). **120 Corbis:** Ed Murray / Star Ledger (clb). **Getty Images:** Yoshikazu Tsuno / AFP (tr). **MIT Media Lab :** (tl). **Used with permission, GM Media Archives.:** Jason Cohn / Carnegie Mellon Tartan Racing (br). **121 Corbis:** Ina Fassbender / X00970 / Reuters (b). **Getty Images:** Ben Hider (tr). **Science Photo Library:** Sam Ogden (tl). **122 Getty Images:** Philippe Lopez / AFP (bc). **123 Corbis:** Car Culture (c). **Getty Images:** Yoshikazu Tsuno / AFP (tr). **Science Photo Library:** Peter Menzel (bl). **124 Associated Press AP:** USAF (tr). **Corbis:** Yuriko Nakao / Reuters (br). **Dounreay Site Restoration Ltd:** (br). **Science Photo Library:** Pascal Goetgheluck (cla). **125 Corbis:** Narong Sangnak / Epa (crb). **Department of Mechanical and Aerospace Engineering at North Carolina State University:** (tr). **Reuters:** Issei Kato IK / TY (bc); Radovan Stoklasa (tl). **Science Photo Library:** Sam Ogden (tl). **129 NASA:** JPL (crb); JPL / Cornell University / Maas Digital (br); JPL-Caltech / Cornell (bc). **Science Photo Library:** NASA / JPL-CALTECH / CORNELL (cra). **130 Science Photo Library:** Eye Of Science (bl). **134 akg-images:** RIA Nowost (h). **The Bridgeman Art Library:** CNAM, Conservatoire National des Arts et Metiers, Paris / Giraudon (a). **Computer History Museum:** (i, j); Mark Richards (c). **Corbis:** Bettmann (f); Lowell Georgia (e). **Science Photo Library:** Peter Menzel (d). **135 Cody Images:** (c). **Corbis:** Gary I Rothstein / Epa (e); Toshiyuki Aizawa / Reuters (i); SSPL (b). **iRobot Corporation:** (j). **Rex Features:** (d); Everett Collection (tl); Times Newspapers Ltd (a). **Science Photo Library:** Mauro Fermariello (h); Peter Menzel (br). **136 Corbis:** Stoyan Nenov / X01507 (cb). **Getty Images:** Time & Life Pictures (tc). **iRobot Corporation:** (cra). **Science Photo Library:** Volker Steger (bc); Victor Habbick Visions (br). **137 Alamy Images:** Emmanuel Lattes (cra). **Corbis:** Heide Benser (tr). **Getty Images:** Robyn Beck / AFP (tl); Kevin Winter (bc). **Science Photo Library:** Studio Macbeth

**Front jacket: Alamy / Hugh Threlfall** (tl); Sony Computer Entertainment (tr); **Corbis / Road and Track / Transtock /** (br); **ICHIRO / Getty Images** (br); **Fotolia / jirkacafa** (bl); **Fotolia / sharpnose** (bl)